Zionism Is Bullshit

Selected Speeches, Interviews and Writings
Volume I

Craig Murray

Atholl Publishing

Copyright © Craig Murray 2017
All Rights Reserved
The moral right of the author has been asserted

Atholl Publishing
21 Sinclair Gardens
London W11 9RD

No part of this book may be reproduced or transmitted in any form except by permission, apart from reasonable quotations to be used in review or discussion.

Typeset in Gentium Book.
ISBN 978-1548026370

Zionism is Bullshit

Craig Murray

Foreword By Kirsten MacDonald

Within the space of a single year, Craig Murray went from being a British Ambassador to describing his occupation as a professional dissident.

Tony Blair's premiership was an extraordinary time. It represented the abandonment by the official party of the "left" in the UK to the ideology of neo-liberalism. It also represented a complete commitment to aggressive foreign policy. Tony Blair engaged in more wars than any other British Prime Minister since the heyday of the Empire.

This was accompanied by the "War on Terror", a period where the media whipped up fears of terrorist attack and government passed an entire series of measures limiting civil liberties. There was a real sense that society was changing permanently to accept a more authoritarian form of government.

Craig Murray was a most improbable focus of resistance to this change. An old fashioned character still given to wearing three piece suits, he regarded himself more as a liberal than a socialist. His political gestures were sometimes Quixotic, for example in standing as an independent candidate against Jack Straw in his Blackburn election in the 2005 general election.

But a combination of his patent honesty, muscular logic and fluent writing style gradually found its audience.

On Murray's part, we could discern a series of influences that were pushing him ineluctably to the left.

Firstly, his anti war instincts drove him into the orbit of the Stop the War campaign. Many of his speeches in this period were given alongside Tony Benn and Jeremy Corbyn.

Secondly, his concern for freedom of information left him exasperated with attempts to censor his memoir,

Murder in Samarkand. He saw himself as a whistleblower and began contact with Wikileaks.

Thirdly, his experience of the persecution of Muslims in Uzbekistan led him to compare that with the impact of the anti-terror legislation on Muslim communities in the UK.

Finally, he was horrified by the growth of wealth inequality in the UK and end of state provision of many services, and particularly at the introduction of university tuition fees.

While not a major political figure, he is an interesting and a prescient one and can be seen as a precursor to the current age of insurgency politics. In studying his work for a university project, I therefore decided a collection might be useful to future researchers of this period.

I have tidied up some speech transcripts a little. I have tried to select material that shows the development of positions over time. This material covers the first two years after Murray left government employment, 2005-7. I hope either I or another researcher will follow up with future volumes.

Kirsten MacDonald
University of Illinois 2017

Zionism is Bullshit

Zionism is Bullshit

Speech before 200,000 people at the Stop the Gaza Massacre Demonstration, London 10 January 2009. Tony Benn, Jeremy Corbyn and George Galloway also spoke.

We stand here today because of the shame that Israel has brought upon mankind by its murderous attack upon the citizens of Gaza and the war crimes it has committed. But today is also a day I am proud. I am proud because for every Palestinian child that has been murdered, 2,000 people have taken to the streets of London to protest against that death.

I am ashamed of my former colleagues, and the diplomatic maneuvering that is going on to delay a ceasefire until the Palestinian people are blackmailed into dropping their resistance and accepting the existence of the state of Israel.

I do not accept the existence of the state of Israel any more than I accepted the existence of apartheid South Africa. Israel is based on ethnic cleansing, on racism.

Every day, 100 times a day, we are seeing pictures of Sderot, and being told that the people of that village live under fear of rocket attack. Not one time has it been said on television that Sderot was a Palestinian village until it was stolen from the Palestinian people. Not one time!

We stand together with the people of Palestine. We stand for a Palestine which is one country, not tiny homelands, surrounded, walled off, and deprived of supplies and water. We stand against racism.

Zionism is bullshit. 3,000 years ago my Celtic ancestors were throwing offerings into the lakes of Switzerland. Can I go and claim Switzerland? Nonsense! Nonsense! We stand for a single, united Palestine. Thank you.

Ceasefire Now Demonstration

Speech to 120,000 people at the demonstration against the Israeli invasion of Lebanon, Parliament Square, 6 August 2006

I today am deeply ashamed of the country which I used to serve.

I am ashamed we have sold out our foreign policy to Bush and we have joined an American/British/Israeli axis to bring unending war and conflict in the Middle East. How can this have happened in this country?

But I see hope. When I look over this crowd – you can't see yourselves – from up here, you go on and on back to Trafalgar Square. Every race, every ethnicity, every religion, you are typical of Great Britain, and when Lebanon bleeds, we bleed for them!

We will not stop. We will not allow our government to continue to send bombs and missiles to Israel, while condemning Hezbollah for the tiny amount they can do in retaliation. We will not stop.

Tony Blair has got British diplomats at the United Nations to block any resolution calling for an immediate ceasefire. That is a crime! It is directly causing the death of thousands of innocent women and children.

Tony Blair has canceled his holiday. He has canceled his holiday so he can continue to work against a ceasefire. Listen Tony. Go! It's OK, you can go on holiday. We don't need you.

You don't need to stay with Rupert Murdoch. You don't need to stay with Silvio Berlusconi. We have a very comfortable cell for you at the International War Crimes Tribunal in the Hague, next to your good friend George Bush.

We want to see Israel out of Lebanon, the United States out of Iraq, and Tony Blair out of Downing Street.

Time to Go Demonstration

On 23 September 2006 Craig Murray gave this speech to 50,000 people protesting against the occupation of Iraq outside the Labour Party conference.

When the Labour party gathers here at Manchester for its annual conference, it is a shameful fact that will be the biggest gathering of war criminals in British history, because they are all guilty. They are all guilty of launching the illegal war on Iraq.

It was a cabinet decision. When they went to war on the basis of lies, when they went to war illegally without the consent of the United Nations Security Council, they permanently damaged the authority of the United Nations, and they have dragged the name of the United Kingdom into the mud as violators of human rights, not upholders of human rights. That is appalling.

It's not just Blair. It's not just Blair. They all voted for that war as a cabinet, the Labour members of Parliament, the majority of them went through the lobby to vote for the war.

When they eventually found out about the lies, did they act then to remove Blair? No! By hanging on to office, by clinging on to their ministerial jobs, they have taken the guilt upon themselves.

Every member of the Labour Party has hands which are stained with blood of Afghan children, of Iraqi children, and Lebanese children.

These people's hands are stained with blood. And when Blair speaks, when they applaud afterwards, that blood will spread to stain their faces, the conference hall, and to cover this fair city of Manchester, which is crying shame at these criminals in its midst.

We, the people, reject them. We reject the policy of continual war, we reject the attack on civil liberties in

this country, and it is time not only for Blair to go, but for the whole, damned, Labour Party to go.
Thank you.

Speech on Receiving the Sam Adams Award for Integrity

The Sam Adams Award is named after a CIA analyst who refused to downgrade estimates of "enemy" strength during the Vietnam War in order to please the Pentagon. It is given to those who show integrity in secret intelligence work. Craig Murray received the award in New York on 1 May 2006

Thank you Ann, and thank you to the associates of Samuel Adams. I'm deeply grateful and deeply touched. I am especially grateful for the candlestick because since I lost my job I can't afford to pay the electricity bill!

I will only say a very few brief words because I am testifying in an hour or so's time so you will see quite enough of me. But I'm absolutely delighted to receive the award which celebrates a great man, Sam Adams, and which has been received by so many people who in many cases were much braver and more honorable than I.

I would like to say something about the advance of evil and how easily it advances. I genuinely at no stage felt I was doing anything either heroic or exceptional. When I came across cases of people being boiled alive, cases of daughters being raped in front of their fathers, cases of torture of children, and the fact that we were receiving intelligence from those torture sessions, it seemed to me axiomatic that anyone brought up in the United States or the United Kingdom would believe their overriding and only duty was to stop it. And, perhaps naively, when I started trying to stop it internally, I actually believed that this must be the work of renegade people at lower levels and that once senior politicians in the UK and US knew what was happening, they would stop it.

I was quickly disillusioned. I discovered this part of a

wider international policy of the use of torture in the pursuit of the war on terror. It was a terrible moment for me. I discovered that the system and the country I'd served my whole life didn't stand for what I believed it did. And I went to meetings with colleagues of mine. People I had known for over 20 years. Ordinary nice people who were setting down on paper strategies by which what we were doing could be said not to circumvent the UN convention against torture. And I was looking at them thinking, "I know you. I know you. We've drunk together. We've played golf together. You are setting up justification for torture. How did this come about?"

This may sound exaggerated. But it isn't. At that moment I understood how some civil servant ended up writing out the orders for cattle trucks to go to Auschwitz, and felt they were only "doing their job." And ladies and gentlemen, that is what we face now: the flight toward fascism.

I am delighted to receive the award. Delighted to make the acquaintance of such good people. I find it's a shame that we have now reached a stage where people like Ray, and Ann, and Scott Ritter, the real patriots who stand for the values that were supposed to underpin the states we live in, the real patriots, are those who are condemned as traitors, and people who dress themselves in flag of patriotism are the real traitors to Western values. Thank you very much indeed."

Three Telegrams

These are official diplomatic communications which Craig Murray as Ambassador to Uzbekistan sent to Foreign Secretary Jack Straw, protesting at UK and US support for the dictatorial regime. Murray particularly objected to the use by the CIA and MI6 of intelligence gained from Uzbekistan's notorious torture chambers.

Confidential
FM Tashkent
TO FCO, Cabinet Office, DFID, MODUK, OSCE Posts, Security Council Posts
16 September 02
SUBJECT: US/Uzbekistan: Promoting Terrorism
SUMMARY
US plays down human rights situation in Uzbekistan. A dangerous policy: increasing repression combined with poverty will promote Islamic terrorism. Support to Karimov regime a bankrupt and cynical policy.
DETAIL
The Economist of 7 September states: "Uzbekistan, in particular, has jailed many thousands of moderate Islamists, an excellent way of converting their families and friends to extremism." The Economist also spoke of "the growing despotism of Mr Karimov" and judged that "the past year has seen a further deterioration of an already grim human rights record". I agree.

Between 7,000 and 10,000 political and religious prisoners are currently detained, many after trials before kangaroo courts with no representation. Terrible torture is commonplace: the EU is currently considering a demarche over the terrible case of two Muslims tortured to death in jail apparently with boiling water. Two leading dissidents, Elena Urlaeva and Larissa

Vdovna, were two weeks ago committed to a lunatic asylum, where they are being drugged, for demonstrating on human rights. Opposition political parties remain banned. There is no doubt that September 11 gave the pretext to crack down still harder on dissent under the guise of counter-terrorism.

Yet on 8 September the US State Department certified that Uzbekistan was improving in both human rights and democracy, thus fulfilling a constitutional requirement and allowing the continuing disbursement of $140 million of US aid to Uzbekistan this year. Human Rights Watch immediately published a commendably sober and balanced rebuttal of the State Department claim.

Again we are back in the area of the US accepting sham reform [a reference to my previous telegram on the economy]. In August media censorship was abolished, and theoretically there are independent media outlets, but in practice there is absolutely no criticism of President Karimov or the central government in any Uzbek media. State Department call this self-censorship: I am not sure that is a fair way to describe an unwillingness to experience the brutal methods of the security services.

Similarly, following US pressure when Karimov visited Washington, a human rights NGO has been permitted to register. This is an advance, but they have little impact given that no media are prepared to cover any of their activities or carry any of their statements.

The final improvement State quote is that in one case of murder of a prisoner the police involved have been prosecuted. That is an improvement, but again related to the Karimov visit and does not appear to presage a general change of policy. On the latest cases of torture deaths the Uzbeks have given the OSCE an incredible explanation, given the nature of the injuries, that the victims died in a fight between prisoners.

But allowing a single NGO, a token prosecution of police officers and a fake press freedom cannot possibly outweigh the huge scale of detentions, the torture and the secret executions. President Karimov has admitted to 100 executions a year but human rights groups believe there are more. Added to this, all opposition parties remain banned (the President got a 98% vote) and the Internet is strictly controlled. All Internet providers must go through a single government server and access is barred to many sites including all dissident and opposition sites and much international media (including, ironically, waronterrorism. com). This is in essence still a totalitarian state: there is far less freedom than still prevails, for example, in Mugabe's Zimbabwe. A Movement for Democratic Change or any judicial independence would be impossible here.

Karimov is a dictator who is committed to neither political nor economic reform. The purpose of his regime is not the development of his country but the diversion of economic rent to his oligarchic supporters through government controls. As a senior Uzbek academic told me privately, there is more repression here now than in Brezhnev's time. The US are trying to prop up Karimov economically and to justify this support they need to claim that a process of economic and political reform is underway. That they do so claim is either cynicism or self-delusion.

This policy is doomed to failure. Karimov is driving this resource-rich country towards economic ruin like an Abacha. And the policy of increasing repression aimed indiscriminately at pious Muslims, combined with a deepening poverty, is the most certain way to ensure continuing support for the Islamic Movement of Uzbekistan. They have certainly been decimated and disorganised in Afghanistan, and Karimov's repression may keep the lid on for years - but pressure is building and could ultimately explode.

I quite understand the interest of the US in strategic airbases and why they back Karimov, but I believe US policy is misconceived. In the short term it may help fight terrorism but in the medium term it will promote it, as the Economist points out. And it can never be right to lower our standards on human rights. There is a complex situation in Central Asia and it is wrong to look at it only through a prism picked up on September 12. Worst of all is what appears to be the philosophy underlying the current US view of Uzbekistan: that September 11 divided the World into two camps in the "War against Terrorism" and that Karimov is on "our" side.

If Karimov is on "our" side, then this war cannot be simply between the forces of good and evil. It must be about more complex things, like securing the long-term US military presence in Uzbekistan. I silently wept at the 11 September commemoration here. The right words on New York have all been said. But last week was also another anniversary - the US-led overthrow of Salvador Allende in Chile. The subsequent dictatorship killed, dare I say it, rather more people than died on September 11. Should we not remember then also, and learn from that too? I fear that we are heading down the same path of US-sponsored dictatorship here. It is ironic that the beneficiary is perhaps the most unreformed of the World's old communist leaders.

We need to think much more deeply about Central Asia. It is easy to place Uzbekistan in the "too difficult" tray and let the US run with it, but I think they are running in the wrong direction. We should tell them of the dangers we see. Our policy is theoretically one of engagement, but in practice this has not meant much. Engagement makes sense, but it must mean grappling with the problems, not mute collaboration. We need to start actively to state a distinctive position on democracy and human rights, and press for a realistic view to be taken in the IMF. We should continue to resist pressures to start a bilateral DFID programme, unless channeled non-governmentally, and not restore ECGD cover despite the constant lobbying. We should not invite Karimov to the UK. We should step up our public diplomacy effort, stressing democratic values, including more resources from the British Council. We should increase support to human rights activists, and strive for contact with non-official Islamic groups.

Above all we need to care about the 22 million Uzbek people, suffering from poverty and lack of freedom. They are not just pawns in the new Great Game.
MURRAY

*****

Confidential
Fm Tashkent
To FCO
18 March 2003
SUBJECT: US FOREIGN POLICY
SUMMARY

1. As seen from Tashkent, US policy is not much focused on democracy or freedom. It is about oil, gas and hegemony. In Uzbekistan the US pursues those ends through supporting a ruthless dictatorship. We must not close our eyes to uncomfortable truth.
DETAIL
   2. Last year the US gave half a billion dollars in aid to Uzbekistan, about a quarter of it military aid. Bush and Powell repeatedly hail Karimov as a friend and ally. Yet this regime has at least seven thousand prisoners of conscience; it is a one party state without freedom of speech, without freedom of media, without freedom of

movement, without freedom of assembly, without freedom of religion. It practices, systematically, the most hideous tortures on thousands. Most of the population live in conditions precisely analogous with medieval serfdom.

3. Uzbekistan's geo-strategic position is crucial. It has half the population of the whole of Central Asia. It alone borders all the other states in a region which is important to future Western oil and gas supplies. It is the regional military power. That is why the US is here, and here to stay. Contractors at the US military bases are extending the design life of the buildings from ten to twenty five years.

4. Democracy and human rights are, despite their protestations to the contrary, in practice a long way down the US agenda here. Aid this year will be slightly less, but there is no intention to introduce any meaningful conditionality. Nobody can believe this level of aid - more than US aid to all of West Africa - is related to comparative developmental need as opposed to political support for Karimov. While the US makes token and low-level references to human rights to appease domestic opinion, they view Karimov's vicious regime as a bastion against fundamentalism. He - and they - are in fact creating fundamentalism. When the US gives this much support to a regime that tortures people to death for having a beard or praying five times a day, is it any surprise that Muslims come to hate the West?

5. I was stunned to hear that the US had pressured the EU to withdraw a motion on Human Rights in Uzbekistan which the EU was tabling at the UN Commission for Human Rights in Geneva. I was most unhappy to find that we are helping the US in what I can only call this cover-up. I am saddened when the US constantly quote fake improvements in human rights in Uzbekistan, such

as the abolition of censorship and Internet freedom, which quite simply have not happened (I see these are quoted in the draft EBRD strategy for Uzbekistan, again I understand at American urging).

6. From Tashkent it is difficult to agree that we and the US are activated by shared values. Here we have a brutal US sponsored dictatorship reminiscent of Central and South American policy under previous US Republican administrations. I watched George Bush talk today of Iraq and "dismantling the apparatus of terror? removing the torture chambers and the rape rooms". Yet when it comes to the Karimov regime, systematic torture and rape appear to be treated as peccadilloes, not to affect the relationship and to be downplayed in international fora. Double standards? Yes.

7. I hope that once the present crisis is over we will make plain to the US, at senior level, our serious concern over their policy in Uzbekistan.

MURRAY

*****

CONFIDENTIAL
FM TASHKENT
TO IMMEDIATE FCO
TELNO 63
OF 220939 JULY 04
INFO IMMEDIATE DFID, ISLAMIC POSTS, MOD, OSCE POSTS UKDEL EBRD LONDON, UKMIS GENEVA, UKMIS MEW YORK
SUBJECT: RECEIPT OF INTELLIGENCE OBTAINED UNDER TORTURE
SUMMARY

1. We receive intelligence obtained under torture from the Uzbek intelligence services, via the US. We should stop. It is bad information anyway. Tortured dupes are forced to sign up to confessions showing what the Uzbek

government wants the US and UK to believe, that they and we are fighting the same war against terror.

2. I gather a recent London interdepartmental meeting considered the question and decided to continue to receive the material. This is morally, legally and practically wrong. It exposes as hypocritical our post Abu Ghraib pronouncements and fatally undermines our moral standing. It obviates my efforts to get the Uzbek government to stop torture they are fully aware our intelligence community laps up the results.

3. We should cease all co-operation with the Uzbek Security Services they are beyond the pale. We indeed need to establish an SIS presence here, but not as in a friendly state.

DETAIL

4. In the period December 2002 to March 2003 I raised several times the issue of intelligence material from the Uzbek security services which was obtained under torture and passed to us via the CIA. I queried the legality, efficacy and morality of the practice.

5. I was summoned to the UK for a meeting on 8 March 2003. Michael Wood gave his legal opinion that it was not illegal to obtain and to use intelligence acquired by torture. He said the only legal limitation on its use was that it could not be used in legal proceedings, under Article 15 of the UN Convention on Torture.

6. On behalf of the intelligence services, Matthew Kydd said that they found some of the material very useful indeed with a direct bearing on the war on terror. Linda Duffield said that she had been asked to assure me that my qualms of conscience were respected and understood.

7. Sir Michael Jay's circular of 26 May stated that there was a reporting obligation on us to report torture by allies (and I have been instructed to refer to Uzbekistan as such in the context of the war on terror). You, Sir,

have made a number of striking, and I believe heartfelt, condemnations of torture in the last few weeks. I had in the light of this decided to return to this question and to highlight an apparent contradiction in our policy. I had intimated as much to the Head of Eastern Department.

8. I was therefore somewhat surprised to hear that without informing me of the meeting, or since informing me of the result of the meeting, a meeting was convened in the FCO at the level of Heads of Department and above, precisely to consider the question of the receipt of Uzbek intelligence material obtained under torture. As the office knew, I was in London at the time and perfectly able to attend the meeting. I still have only gleaned that it happened.

9. I understand that the meeting decided to continue to obtain the Uzbek torture material. I understand that the principal argument deployed was that the intelligence material disguises the precise source, ie it does not ordinarily reveal the name of the individual who is tortured. Indeed this is true - the material is marked with a euphemism such as "From detainee debriefing." The argument runs that if the individual is not named, we cannot prove that he was tortured.

10. I will not attempt to hide my utter contempt for such casuistry, nor my shame that I work in and organisation where colleagues would resort to it to justify torture. I have dealt with hundreds of individual cases of political or religious prisoners in Uzbekistan, and I have met with very few where torture, as defined in the UN convention, was not employed. When my then DHM raised the question with the CIA head of station 15 months ago, he readily acknowledged torture was deployed in obtaining intelligence. I do not think there is any doubt as to the fact

11. The torture record of the Uzbek security services could hardly be more widely known. Plainly there are, at

the very least, reasonable grounds for believing the material is obtained under torture. There is helpful guidance at Article 3 of the UN Convention;

"The competent authorities shall take into account all relevant considerations including, where applicable, the existence in the state concerned of a consistent pattern of gross, flagrant or mass violations of human rights."

While this article forbids extradition or deportation to Uzbekistan, it is the right test for the present question also.

12. On the usefulness of the material obtained, this is irrelevant. Article 2 of the Convention, to which we are a party, could not be plainer:

"No exceptional circumstances whatsoever, whether a state of war or a threat of war, internal political instability or any other public emergency, may be invoked as a justification of torture."

13. Nonetheless, I repeat that this material is useless - we are selling our souls for dross. It is in fact positively harmful. It is designed to give the message the Uzbeks want the West to hear. It exaggerates the role, size, organisation and activity of the IMU and its links with Al Qaida. The aim is to convince the West that the Uzbeks are a vital cog against a common foe, that they should keep the assistance, especially military assistance, coming, and that they should mute the international criticism on human rights and economic reform.

14. I was taken aback when Matthew Kydd said this stuff was valuable. Sixteen months ago it was difficult to argue with SIS in the area of intelligence assessment. But post Butler we know, not only that they can get it wrong on even the most vital and high profile issues, but that they have a particular yen for highly coloured material which exaggerates the threat. That is precisely what the Uzbeks give them. Furthermore MI6 have no operative within a thousand miles of me and certainly no expertise

that can come close to my own in making this assessment.

15. At the Khuderbegainov trial I met an old man from Andizhan. Two of his children had been tortured in front of him until he signed a confession on the family's links with Bin Laden. Tears were streaming down his face. I have no doubt they had as much connection with Bin Laden as I do. This is the standard of the Uzbek intelligence services.

16. I have been considering Michael Wood's legal view, which he kindly gave in writing. I cannot understand why Michael concentrated only on Article 15 of the Convention. This certainly bans the use of material obtained under torture as evidence in proceedings, but it does not state that this is the sole exclusion of the use of such material.

17. The relevant article seems to me Article 4, which talks of complicity in torture. Knowingly to receive its results appears to be at least arguable as complicity. It does not appear that being in a different country to the actual torture would preclude complicity. I talked this over in a hypothetical sense with my old friend Prof Francois Hampson, I believe an acknowledged World authority on the Convention, who said that the complicity argument and the spirit of the Convention would be likely to be winning points. I should be grateful to hear Michael's views on this.

18. It seems to me that there are degrees of complicity and guilt, but being at one or two removes does not make us blameless. There are other factors. Plainly it was a breach of Article 3 of the Convention for the coalition to deport detainees back here from Baghram, but it has been done. That seems plainly complicit.

19. This is a difficult and dangerous part of the World. Dire and increasing poverty and harsh repression are undoubtedly turning young people here towards radical

Islam. The Uzbek government are thus creating this threat, and perceived US support for Karimov strengthens anti-Western feeling. SIS ought to establish a presence here, but not as partners of the Uzbek Security Services, whose sheer brutality puts them beyond the pale.
MURRAY

Speech to the University of York

On resigning from the FCO Craig Murray embarked on a speaking tour of universities, in which he related his experiences in Uzbekistan to the immorality of wider Western policy in the "War on Terror". This speech was delivered to the University of York on 24 February 2005.

I'm going to start with a brief anecdote from my career. I was in the diplomatic service for twenty years after leaving university in 1984. I worked my way up the ranks until I became Ambassador to Uzbekistan in 2002 until October 2004 when I was sacked. It had been a good career up until then. I'd like to tell you something from a slightly earlier period in my career. It may not seem immediately relevant but later on you'll hopefully understand its relevance.

I was first secretary at the British Embassy in Warsaw in the mid-90's. I was in charge of the political and economic section of the British embassy in Warsaw. There was another first secretary in the Embassy who officially did a similar job to me, but in fact he was MI6. I had a friend in Warsaw who was a Polish restaurateur; he owned and ran the best restaurant in Poland at that time. He also ate at a lot of government functions. He was a kind of society figure, he'd be invited to political dinner parties, he was a great gossip and purveyor of political tittle-tattle. His name was Stephan. One day I met Stephan and he told me a story about the then Polish Prime Minister- Joseph Alexis and I was able to say to Stephan - that's not true, it didn't happen- I was there, that isn't what he said. 'Alright' said Stephan.

The next day I was at a different restaurant in Warsaw - that's what diplomats do mostly - they sit in restaurants and eat substantial amounts. I was having lunch in another restaurant and I saw Stephan and this other first secretary Tom ensconced at a table on the far side of the room. Low and behold the very next day I received on my desk in its striking bright red cover a piece of MI6 intelligence material containing this story about the Polish Prime Minister. And I wrote on it 'This is nonsense, this came from Stephan (and I put his full name) - he told me this too. It's not true, I was there.' And I sent it back to MI6. The result of this was that I was formally disciplined for having named the source of the information- which you're never allowed to do. The fact that the information wasn't true at all didn't seem to trouble MI6 in the least. And the sequel is even more interesting.

Two days later I met Stephan again and I said 'Stephan you told Tom that story didn't you?' And he said 'Yeah.' And I said 'but I'd already told you that it wasn't true'- why did you do that? Stephan smiled and said 'well he paid me $8000 for it.' Absolutely true story. It will give you more of an insight into the actual workings of MI6 than James Bond Films ever will. And the relevance of it will perhaps become obvious to you as I carry on with my tale of what happened to me in Uzbekistan. And what I saw in Uzbekistan.

Uzbekistan is a pretty dreadful state. It's immediately North of Afghanistan. It's one of those former Soviet Union States "the stans" that people have difficulty telling apart. It's the largest of them. Its population at 24 million is effectively half the population of central Asia. And Tashkent the capital was the fourth largest city in the Soviet Union. The government is a post-soviet government and the leadership hasn't changed. Islam Karimov the President was the resident of the Uzbek Soviet Socialist Republic and had been for many years. Its well to understand what happened and how the country got independence.

Most of you are probably too young to recall it but there was an attempt at a coup against Gorbachev while he was President of the Soviet Union. They had tanks outside the Russian Parliament- the white house. There was a big stand off - the parliament building was being fired at by the tanks. Yeltsin famously clambered up on the tanks and talked to the soldiers out of supporting the coup which subsequently collapsed. It was the start of Yeltsin's rise to power. Karimov and the other heads of the central Asian states who were politburo members supported the hardliners - supported the hardline communist coup against Gorbachev and were most upset when it failed. Very quickly after the Soviet Union fell apart and the reason they opted for independence was to maintain the soviet system. Plainly Russia was going its own way - Russia was abandoning communism - moving towards market reform and greater political freedom. They didn't want that- they could actually only maintain the soviet system by seceding which is slightly counter-intuitive but that's how it happened.

Now it's very important to understand that because George Bush doesn't understand it. Karimov is now the United States' great friend and ally in the region. And Condoleezza Rice, Colin Powell, Donald Rumsfeld, Dick Cheney - they've all been to visit Uzbekistan. Karimov has been Bush's guest in the White House for tea. When then US treasury secretary O'Neil visited in November 2002 he gave a speech which absolutely sums up the American misconception in that he praised Karimov as one of the people who helped destroy the Soviet Union and bring down the evil empire and said he was a freedom fighter alongside Walesa and Havel. Completely wrong, fundamental misconception of the kind that only an American neo-conservative could come up with.

The Soviet system has been maintained in that there's no private ownership of land - all land is still state owned. There's been very little privatization of industry - and what has been privatized has been privatized into the hands of members of the regime and their families notably into the hands of the daughter of the president. The economy is still very heavily agriculturally based - 60% of the workforce work in agriculture on state farms and agriculture produces about 60% of GDP. Cotton is the biggest single crop - Uzbekistan is the world second largest exporter of cotton.

The cotton is produced on state farms and sold only to state trading companies - they are the monopoly purchasers. The price the companies pay for the cotton is about 3% of the price of cotton in neighboring Kazakhstan where production is private. So that's a pretty good guide to the market price- it's about 3% of the market price. The state trading companies then sell it on to international trading companies at the world price- so as you can imagine their profit margin is absolutely incredible. Not only incredible but totally non-transparent - there are no official statistics - you're not allowed to know revenue is, what expenditure is, where it goes. This of course leads to a tremendous margin for corruption. It's important to understand that western trading companies are involved in that corruption.

How do you make cotton farms produce cotton so cheaply? Well I visited one farm for example with 12000 hectares and 16000 workers. And the workers are $2 a month which is 7 US Cents per working day. The point is this is slave labour. They still have not only exit visas to prevent the population from escaping the country - they still have internal visas. If you are born on an Uzbek state farm you are there for life. You are not allowed to leave and go to another town. So effectively the system is serfdom. Not only that but come the cotton harvest which is harvested by hand in scenes reminiscent of the

American south 150 years ago, others are conscripted in for no money at all to harvest and particularly all university students and all school pupils have to, without pay, harvest cotton for two or three months in the autumn. University students having to go three whole months and live and work in the cotton fields. They have to pick 80 kilos a day each of cotton.

Schoolchildren as young as seven have to do this - they sleep in the fields, they are hardly fed. And no one is paid for it. This really is slave labour on a massive scale. And there is almost no realization of this in the west.

Sadly there is not a great deal that can be done about it other than try and put pressure on the trading companies. None of us know whether the shirt we are wearing contains Uzbek cotton because while the labeling will tell you where the shirt was manufactured it won't tell you where the cotton fibres came from. That's the cotton industry.

Gold is Uzbekistan's second biggest industry. Uzbekistan is the 6th or 7th largest Gold producer in the world. Again it's produced by a state kombinat also one of the worlds leading producers of Uranium. It does not operate as a company in the sense that we understand it. The companies revenues bear no relation whatsoever to its sales or the price of gold. The company gets an allocation of funds to meet its costs from the ministry of finance with which it pays its meager wages and for its equipment and other costs.

The gold is shipped off to Switzerland to be sold. How much is produced is a state secret. The price at which it's sold is a state secret. There's no means of knowing what the revenue was but it's a hell of a lot more than the ministry of finance allocation to the company. The huge profits are what finance the state budget but also the secrecy of it gives tremendous opportunity for stealing. The gold industry in particular is where the bulk of the

President's personal fortune comes from. And he takes according to sources I believe who are in a position to know he takes 10% of the revenue of the gold industry.

Socially and political Uzbekistan is an efficient totalitarian state with no freedom of assembly, no freedom of speech, absolutely no freedom of the media, no freedom of religion, no opposition is allowed to contest elections. The system runs on informants and secret police and torture. Tashkent is a city of just over 2 million people; one telling fact is that there isn't a bookshop in Tashkent, not one in the whole of the city. There are a few stalls that sell old books which occasionally get closed down. But there's no bookshop. Gives you some idea of the poverty of information.

There's no independent media at all. All information is strictly state controlled. When 9/11 happened everywhere in the world within a few hours people were seeing that dreadful event on television screens. In Uzbekistan no news of it was permitted at all for 72 hours after the event and you are talking of a country so remote, so cut off, that that kind of news management can work; people just don't get information.

When I arrived in this country and I'd been there about a fortnight a chap in my political section came and asked if I wanted to go and attend the trial of a dissident. I agreed to go along. The gentleman on trial was a chap called Khuderbegainov. He along with five others were charged with a series, a charge sheet of about 20 crimes. Not all of them were charged with each of the crimes. It was a kind of pick and mix thing. Some were charged with some of them. Three charged with this one, two charged with that one and so on. They were kept in an Iron cage they looked emaciated, they looked bruised. They were surrounded by 17 armed guards. Throughout the trial they were harangued regularly by the judge.

The atmosphere was just awful; it called to mind for me

old television pictures of Nazi show trials. Two comments of the judge stick in my mind and they were typical of the general anti-Islamic tone of his comments. He said "I'm surprised they found the time to do all these evil things when they had to stop and pray five times a day." All the court officials laughed in unison. Similarly he said at one stage "How could you understand each other talking when you all have such long beards".

A jeweler came in who'd been the victim allegedly of an armed robbery. It was alleged that three of the men had robbed him. He was asked to identify the three who had robbed him. I'm not a statistician but the odds against this are extremely high- he managed to choose three of the six who were not charged with robbing him. The judge got very angry at this, read out the names of the three who should have been identified, they stood up and he said "that was the men wasn't it" the witness said "oh yes" and the judge said "let the record show that they were correctly identified". I just find it hard to believe I was there.

And then something happened that put the seal on the nature of the event - what it was designed to show us. An old man came in and he was charged, he had signed a statement saying that two of the accused who were nephews of his were associates of Osama Bin Laden, had been to Afghanistan, and met Bin Laden on a regular basis. He was standing there, and he was an old gentleman, frail and bowed, with a very oriental appearance, a long white beard, and a skull cap. And he was standing there while his sentence was given out, mumbling his answers and suddenly he pulled himself erect looked at the judge in the eye and he said "it's not true- they tortured my children in front of me until I signed this. We are poor farmers, what do we know of Osama Bin Laden? What have I to do with Bin Laden?" He was quickly hustled out by the military. It felt to me that what he was saying was the truth.

At the end of this trial the defendants were all found guilty and some were given death sentences. One of the charges they were involved in was the murder of two policemen. I discovered from Human Rights Watch that a significant number of people 12 or 20 I forget which, had already been convicted of this murder. There was no suggestion that these policemen had been murdered by a mob or that it was a conspiracy. It's simply that when a real crime occurs, like a murder, the Uzbek government uses that to get rid of a lot of dissidents and they don't have any trouble. The other people convicted were not just people in Tashkent- people all round the country had been convicted for this particular murder.

I'll tell you another fact- in Uzbekistan the conviction rate in trials is over 99%. I know this because DFID had a project of putting recording equipment into courtrooms so there could be an official record. Because one of the problems of the system was that nothing the defense said was ever recorded. Several thousand trials had been conducted, that had been recorded. So I asked how many verdicts of not-guilty were there among these trials- the answer was nil. No one had ever been found not-guilty in any of the trials recorded. I raised this with the Uzbek foreign minister and he said to me "you see our system is perfect" "You have a very bad system - in your country innocent people get accused. In our country the innocent are never accused, only the guilty are accused. That's why they are all convicted." This of course left me greatly reassured.

The next day I received from the same member of my political section an envelope. He said you might not want to look at these; this is a case that's come in. I did in the end take the photos out of the envelope. They were photos of a corpse of a gentleman called Avazov. The photos had been brought in by his mother. He was allegedly a member, he probably was, of the Hizb ut Tahrir sect- a rather extreme Muslim sect, though not one that promotes violence. Membership of that sect is itself a crime and he had been put into prison where he had been tortured to sign a recantation of his faith this is something prisoners are very regularly tortured to sign. They have to sign a recantation of faith, an oath of loyalty to the president and then give the names of half a dozen or so of their associates. If you do all that you then have a fair chance of getting out of jail through a presidential amnesty. He had been tortured with a view to signing the recantation along with his colleague Mr Abisov. They had refused and had also refused to cease praying five times a day. As a consequence they had been plunged into a vat of boiling water and had died both of them as a result. I didn't know that at the time, I just saw the photographs of this body in this appalling state; I couldn't work out what could account for it.

I sent it to the pathology department of the University of Glasgow; there were a lot of photographs. The chief pathologist of the University of Glasgow who is now chief pathologist of the United Kingdom wrote that the only explanation for this was "immersion in boiling water". He said it was immersion, not splattering or splashing, because there was a clear tide line around the upper torso and upper limbs. It was also clearly the kind of burning caused by boiling liquid not by flame. The pathologist also found that his fingernails had been pulled out. That clearly took me aback.

Once it became known in Uzbekistan that I was interested in such cases people started coming to my door- both victims and parents of victims and we started to build up a catalogue of these dreadful cases and I can't give you a precise statistic but of those 99% of people convicted well over 90% confess very often to things they didn't do at all. And that extraordinary conviction rate and that extraordinary confession rate is based on these appalling forms of torture and this is in no way isolated- the United Nations special rapporteur on torture came in November 2002 and produced a report in which he said the practice of torture in Uzbekistan was "widespread and systemic" throughout the security services.

When you become an ambassador you pay courtesy calls on your counterparts. I went and I called on the French and the German ambassadors and I said to them 'this is just appalling, I can't believe the things I'm finding here. I'm completely struck by it'. The French ambassador said 'Oh well you shouldn't meet these people if it upsets you'. The German ambassador said 'of course we all know human rights abuses here are very bad, but of course we also know President Karimov is a very close ally of the United States and so we have an agreement that we don't mention it'. I sent a telegram back to London in which I reported he's said this and said that I presumed that there wasn't such an agreement in any formal sense and I had no doubt whatsoever that British ministers wouldn't agree to such a thing and I proposed to start making some speeches and kicking up a fuss about it, which I then did (before they had time to reply). The call I made on the American ambassador was the most interesting. I said that Human Rights Watch were saying that there were some 7000 political prisoners in Uzbekistan. Now by this stage I had started going round towns and villages talking to people. I was trying on each occasion to get an idea of how many political/religious prisoners had been taken in, in that town. In one town in the Ferghana valley they had lost over 300 people out of a population of about 1500. I was forming a view that actually there were an awful lot more than 7000 prisoners. Particularly as the 7000 only included those who were imprisoned on ostensibly political or religious grounds. Whereas many thousands more had narcotics or firearms planted on them. It seems remarkable but almost all political dissidents in Uzbekistan appear to sleep with substantial amounts of narcotics in their bedside cabinet which the police invariably "find".

If you include these people, whom Human Rights Watch don't like to adopt because officially they have been charged with some crime, the number is more like ten to twelve thousand people in jail in Uzbekistan effectively for their beliefs. The American ambassador said to me 'well most of them are Muslims' as thought that explained everything. I said that I didn't think that seemed like particularly good reason why they should be locked up. He said 'But they're extreme Muslims'. I said 'from what I can see there is very little history of political or terrorist violence in Uzbekistan and most of these people are not extreme in the sense that they are advocating violence'. What he said to me was 'We are next door to Afghanistan; we are next door to the Taliban. The kind of society the Taliban impose is itself a form of violence and for example the subjugation of women is itself a form of violence. So if that's what we are holding back, then some reduction of civil liberties in the interim is no bad thing. To which I replied that there was virtually no history of Taliban type Islamic extremism in Uzbekistan and certainly the people I had been meeting were not Taliban type extremists in any sense. Furthermore even if some of these people did propound a Muslim based society, with Sharia law and so on, then as long as they were not advocating violence to achieve it then this was a case of 'well I detest what you say but I will defend your right to say it.' I certainly didn't think there was any excuse at all for throwing them in jail and pulling their fingernails out.

However the Americans were prepared and are prepared to give Karimov a great deal of latitude. To the extent that several hundred million dollars a year in aid goes to Uzbekistan. Since concern has arisen regarding human rights in Uzbekistan the Americans have become much more reluctant to admit the full extent of aid. There is so much coming from different budgets (some of which are hidden) that it is very hard to pin down exactly how much aid Uzbekistan gets from the United States. In December 2002 the US embassy in Uzbekistan put out a press release saying that US aid to Uzbekistan in 2002 was over 500 million dollars. To put that into perspective that is a great deal more than the total aid given by the US to all of West Africa which shows I think that development isn't the criteria. Since then they are much more wary, particularly when it comes to the military and security aid of giving an exact figure. It has probably come down a bit - it is probably now somewhere between 300 and 500 million dollars a year going to prop up the Karimov regime.

Now I said to you before that there's no room for democracy, there was something of a tradition of parties dating back to the pre-Soviet period. There were two parties in Uzbekistan both of which include distinguished dissidents amongst their membership. Both were banned from contesting December's parliamentary elections and I very much doubt anyone here knew this, as there's no way you would, but Uzbekistan held elections on the 26th of December the same day as the Ukraine- both former Soviet republics. In the Uzbek elections opposition parties were not allowed to stand; only parties who supported the President and his program were allowed to stand.

Now we all saw Colin Powell on TV decrying electoral fraud in the Ukraine,talking about the need to spread democracy. The United States said absolutely bugger all about their friend and his rigged election in Uzbekistan, because democracy is not really the agenda. Just as we allegedly went to war with the United States - I thought at the time it was to do with this dodgy dossier of lies on weapons of mass destruction- but apparently it wasn't that at all- it was to impose democracy. How can we do that their when we are backing one of the worlds most vicious dictators in Uzbekistan at the same time? The answer is of course that there is no logic because democracy in Iraq is an excuse for a war designed to promote the hydro-carbon oil and gas interests in the United States- which is also their interest in Uzbekistan.

America has an airbase in Uzbekistan at which there are officially two squadrons of the United States Air force - there is plenty more that they will not tell you about. It is defended by several thousand troops; it was used in operations in Afghanistan. It has now become a permanent installation. It's a vital component in Donald Rumsfeld's concept of what he calls "lilypads" surrounding what he calls "the wider Middle East". This is a series of airbases which the US has access to - the British bases in Cyprus are at the Western end and Uzbekistan is at the eastern end- a series of "lilypads" whereby America can project military power quickly in any of the oil-rich regions of the Middle East.

Just in the last couple of days the go-ahead has been given for the construction of the pipeline to Afghanistan which will bring Central Asia's massive gas reserves out. Uzbekistan while the dominant country in central Asia it does not have the dominant amount of hydro-carbons but in terms of military strength and population it is the dominant regional player and central Asia has enough gas to supply the Western world at present levels of consumption for at least fifty years. So this is all about power play and hydro-carbons and if that power play is best advanced by backing a dictator that's fine so long as no-one knows about it because no-one in the West does know about it. The number of people in the West who already know the things I have told you is extremely small. You're probably the only people in York who know anything about Uzbekistan. The Uzbek's play their part and help the American justification for what they are doing by saying that they are an integral part in the war on terror. The main way they do this is by providing intelligence material linking the Uzbek opposition to Al-Qaeda.

In November 2002 I was sitting looking through MI6 intelligence material I saw some of which the markings indicated it was a re-release of CIA material passed on from another security service - from the text it was plain that was Uzbek. There were two intelligence reports; one about a threat to Samarkand - a city in Uzbekistan- from Tajik militants in the hills- Islamic militants who were supposedly going to sweep down and attack the city. We happened to know that this just wasn't true- the defense attach? had been there, we knew the places, there weren't training camps where it said there were. The second one was talking of the links between some Uzbek opposition group with Al-Qaeda and Osama Bin Laden - it was just the same formula that I had seen before. And I started thinking now has this been got through torture? How did it get here? Where did it come from? So I said to my deputy 'I want to go back to London and complain about this but I don't want to make a fool of myself so could you go and see the Americans because it's possible that they have a protocol in place to make sure that any information passed on by the Uzbek's doesn't come from torture. Perhaps Americans have to be present during Uzbek interrogation if the material is to be used by the Americans.'

This of course is before Abu Ghraib when I rather naively felt that having Americans present at the interrogation would prevent people being tortured as opposed to helping to facilitate it. So She went and saw the CIA head of station in Tashkent and said to him' my boss has been worried that this intelligence might be obtained by torture' and he said to her 'well it probably is obtained by torture - we don't see that as a problem' She came back and reported to me so I went back to London saying' This material is nonsense and probably obtained by torture' London did not actually reply.

I went back in February saying much the same thing and they called me back to a meeting in March 2003 where the foreign office legal advisor Sir Michael Wood said that it was not illegal to obtain or use intelligence material that had been got under torture. If you read the UN convention against torture it didn't say you couldn't do it- it said you couldn't torture people, it said you couldn't use material obtained by torture in court- it didn't say that you couldn't go to someone else who'd tortured someone, get the torture material off him and use it. I think it didn't say it because it didn't need to be said. Also he was ignoring article four of the convention which talks about complicity in torture. Basically if you are regularly obtaining material from a security service that is routinely practicing torture and you have a system of getting that material again and again then you become complicit. The foreign office argues to this day that it's OK to get the stuff. The official line is 'we do not torture and we do not instigate torture but it would be irresponsible to ignore material which is relevant to the war on terror.'

If you really push them they'll say 'what if the Uzbek's suddenly gave us information that an airplane was about to crash into Canary Wharf? Would you really want us to ignore the information?' This of course discounts the fact the information's all not true anyway. It's all nonsense. It would be impossible through all that dross to pick out the true bits. I must admit I was completely flabbergasted, again possibly naively. I thought 'we're getting this material from people who have been tortured; obviously people in London don't realize that. When I point it out to them they will want to stop.'

This of course was not the case. At this stage they got very annoyed, they seemed particularly annoyed that I was saying that the intelligence wasn't any good. I don't think I helped myself by pointing out that the dossier on Weapons of Mass Destruction was rubbish too. They seemed very fond of intelligence that was rubbish. So they didn't find that very conciliatory. But it's a very important point; you have to ask yourself why do the intelligence services like material?

I told you the story of my mate Tom and Stephan; the dossier on weapons of mass destruction which contained 152 articles all of which turned out to be untrue, every bloody single one of them. Almost all of those had come from paying wadges of cash to dodgy informants. Not only that they were getting the information they wanted to hear. They wanted to hear that Saddam Hussein was a terrible threat; they want to hear that the opposition in Uzbekistan are all linked to Al-Qaeda and all want to blow up Canary Wharf. Why? Well if you're going to be totally cynical you'd say that whether subconsciously or not the truth is the bigger the threat out there the more we need the security services, the more they need massive budgets and resources and pay increases and toys to play with. And you have to ask 'who benefits?' Well they benefit, they benefit. They also benefit government by providing these excuses for Tony Blair to stand up in the house of commons and say 'because I am responsible for the safety of all the people in the UK we can abolish freedoms that have existed in this country since Magna Carta. They benefit from this edifice of lies, and lies gained through torture. There are people still today in Belmarsh prison who have been in there for three years without charge, without trial. Without even being told what they are accused of, on the basis of intelligence material.

Now I only saw it in Uzbekistan. If I'd been the ambassador to Saudi Arabia, the ambassador in Egypt or in Syria and a number of other countries I would also have been seeing material obtained through torture. Furthermore there is increasing evidence that the United States is shipping people from country's that don't practice torture to those that do in order to get them tortured. A kind of sub-contracting of torture. So this is the kind of rubbish evidence that the government is using to lock people up in this country and it seems to me that we have lost all perspective of legality in international relations. In November, this country - the United Kingdom - was criticized by the UN committee against torture in Geneva. How did we let that happen? We entered an illegal war against Iraq, expressly against the wishes of the Security Council. We didn't even bother to go for a second resolution because we had checked and we knew we were going to lose the vote, so we went to war without it. Kofi Annan has subsequently said that that war was illegal. And I don't think you will find many academics or public international lawyers that will disagree. Legal opinion is very heavily on the side of the view that that war was an illegal war.

We have abandoned morality; we seem to have no shame at the fact that we presented to the Security Council a dossier full of actual lies. What has happened to this country? I used to enjoy my job, I was proud to represent this country, I was proud to represent a country that I thought stood for human rights. And that stood for the rule of law that stood for the United Nations, stood for fairness in international relations. And we seem to have thrown that entirely out of the window in favor of a policy that says 'the United States is the world's only superpower - they can do what the hell they want and we'll be OK cos we'll be their best mate. That's no basis for foreign policy at all.

I think it's absolutely necessary for people of good will in this country to really start to kick up a fuss about it. And you've got a chance because there's a general election coming. It's imperative that when you get back to your homes, to your constituencies that you find candidates who are willing to take these issues on. If they are in the Labour party you ask why the hell they haven't left the Labour party. They can be liberal democrats, greens whoever, but we have to try to reinvigorate the democratic process and get people interested. I'm actually going to go to Blackburn and stand against Jack Straw as an independent in order to raise public awareness of these issues as far as I can. 'The Guardian' are going to publish my campaign diary which will give an opportunity to get some of these issues aired. But it's no good just saying 'oh yeah, it's terrible' you need to get out there and do something, because there's a real danger that in a few years time if we continue this slide towards authoritarianism and this slide towards supporting an international order based on nothing but a single superpower that in a few years time this won't be a country that any of you will be able to be proud of.

Thank you.

Interview With Radio Free Europe

In this interview with Prague based Radio Free Europe/Radio Liberty on 18 February 2005, Craig Murray set out why he had decided to stand for election against Jack Straw in the 2005 General Election.

(RFE/RL) -- Craig Murray may be one of Britain's least diplomatic diplomats in recent memory. While ambassador to Tashkent, he spoke publicly about repression and the lack of democratic freedoms in Uzbekistan. Last year he accused the United States and United Kingdom of using intelligence gained from people tortured in Uzbekistan. And in a widely published speech in November, he criticized the United States for helping prop up what he called President Islam Karimov's "brutal" regime. Murray was suspended from his post in October 2004 and has now taken severance pay -- moves the British Foreign Office has said are not connected with his outspoken views. He now plans to run against British Foreign Secretary Jack Straw in Britain's Parliamentary election, expected in May.

RFE/RL: What's prompted you to stand against Jack Straw in the upcoming general election?

Murray: I think that under this government Britain has moved away from the basic principles that governed foreign policy for many years, in particular support for the United Nations, support for the role of international law. And that's really quite a serious step which the British people didn't approve of, people didn't approve of us entering into an illegal war against Iraq without the sanction of the UN Security Council. So I'm trying to bring that home to the foreign secretary, because he obviously carries the responsibility for foreign policy.

RFE/RL: Are you hoping to emulate Martin Bell [a former

British journalist who entered politics in order to defeat a member of parliament embroiled in a corruption scandal] or is winning not the point?

Murray: I'm hoping to do a "Martin Bell" in the sense that I want to make the illegal war on Iraq, the government's attacks on human rights at home, its failure to support human rights abroad -- I'm hoping to make those key issues which get more national attention than they would otherwise. Martin Bell did the same two elections ago for the issue of sleaze, and concentrated media attention on that. I'm hoping to concentrate media attention on the issues of legality and foreign policy. So I'm hoping to emulate him in that sense, bring media attention on a relevant issue. Obviously I'd like to emulate him in terms of being elected, but that's entirely up to the voters of Blackburn [Straw's constituency].

RFE/RL: And you are including in those issues that you want to highlight the U.K.'s acceptance of intelligence gained under torture overseas?

Murray: That's one of the key issues I will highlight, the fact that Jack Straw has personally sanctioned the use by the U.K. of intelligence materials obtained under torture. I came across it in Uzbekistan, but exactly the same thing is happening in Egypt, Saudi Arabia, many many countries. What is worse, people have been able to be locked up here in the U.K., detained without trial, on the basis of such intelligence, which is really a dreadful scandal. I will by trying to highlight that in the election campaign.

RFE/RL: What was it that prompted you to speak out about rights abuses while you were ambassador to Uzbekistan?

Murray: I think the brutality in Tashkent was so extreme and so all-pervasive that it was necessary to expose it. I did speak out very strongly, but for example [former U.S. Secretary of State] Madeleine Albright had made a speech in 2000 which was just as strong as anything I ever said about the regime in Tashkent. Sadly, of course, with the coming of the [George W.] Bush administration, America decided it was again going to start backing some nasty dictators who they viewed as on their side, and the American position changed, and the rest of the West was only too eager to fall in behind that noncritical support of [Uzbek President Islam] Karimov. But that was in violation of every international agreement on human rights, and I was only speaking along the lines of accepted British policy.

RFE/RL: What was the reaction of your fellow ambassadors?

Murray: I think they were pretty surprised. When I first arrived in Uzbekistan, as a new ambassador you make courtesy calls on other ambassadors. When I called on other European Union ambassadors and said to them, 'Goodness the human rights situation here is terrible, this is a really nasty dictatorship,' two of them said to me absolutely directly, 'Yes we know, but we don't mention that because they're [Uzbekistan] close allies of the United States.' And there was an understanding among ambassadors in Tashkent that they just pretended not to notice what was going on. That made their lives more comfortable living and working in Tashkent, they weren't people personally fond of confrontations. And I think there was some discomfort and pique that I had brought to public attention issues that they viewed as best swept under the carpet.

RFE/RL: The United States has said it's promoting reforms in Uzbekistan and that it has kept human rights on the agenda, withholding some aid last year because of the poor human rights record. The EU has also spoken in terms of supporting and encouraging reforms. Has this approach brought any results, do you think?

Murray: No, none whatsoever. There isn't any reform

happening. The U.S. sometimes tries to pretend there are bits and pieces of reform. For example, two years ago the U.S. ambassador was loudly proclaiming the abolition of censorship. [the U.S. ambassador said in 2002 he welcomed the move to end official media censorship, but added it was only a first step leading Uzbekistan to an open society.] In fact no such thing has happened, Uzbekistan is still 100 percent censored in its media. And when the State Department cut $12 million of aid last year because of Uzbekistan's appalling human rights record, the Pentagon immediately gave an increase in military aid of more than twice that to make it up. [In August, General Richard Meyers, the chairman of the Joint Chiefs of Staff, announced in Tashkent that Washington would give Uzbekistan an additional $21 million to prevent the proliferation of biological weapons.] I think that the U.S. is in an absolutely disgraceful position with regard to Uzbekistan.

RFE/RL: How should the West treat the Uzbek regime?

Murray: We should treat it as a pariah regime. There is certainly no more freedom in Uzbekistan than there is in Belarus, and the regime in Tashkent is still more vicious and violent than the regime of [Belorussian President Alyaksandr] Lukashenko. And Lukashenko we're quite happy to ostracize and bring sanctions against while we court Karimov. If you take Zimbabwe, which was named as one of [U.S. Secretary of State] Condoleezza Rice's evil dictatorships, I have no time for President [Robert] Mugabe, but there is an opposition in Zimbabwe, and people can, at some risk, go to the polls and vote for an opposition candidate, and they do so. There is an independent judiciary in Zimbabwe whereas there is no such thing in Tashkent. Uzbekistan is certainly in the 'Top 10' for dictatorial regimes in the world and we should treat it as such. We don't have any difficulty treating Mugabe and Lukashenko as pariahs, so why should we not treat Karimov in the same way?

RFE/RL: Do you think you achieved anything by speaking out?

Murray: There are individual cases of people who would be in prison today and possibly would be dead today if we hadn't managed to act and intervene in their cases in Uzbekistan. I think there is much more international attention towards Uzbekistan. I don't believe, for example, that the [U.S.] State Department would have made its token cut in aid if it wasn't for the international attention that the U.K. brought to the human rights violations in Uzbekistan. So I have achieved something in at least raising an awareness of the problem in the world. But plainly I haven't achieved any real reform in Uzbekistan because there is no sign of that.

RFE/RL: Do you have any regrets about what you did?

Murray: Obviously on a personal basis I enormously regret the loss of my career which had been extremely successful in my 20 years at the Foreign Office. I didn't head to Uzbekistan thinking, 'This is a good place to throw my career away.' It wasn't intended. I regret that, but I don't feel I could have done anything else.

The Andizhan Massacre

On 13 May 2005 in Andizhan, Uzbekistan, over 800 peaceful protestors against economic hardship were massacred by government forces – some of them UK trained. It was generally accepted that Craig Murray's warnings had been justified. He wrote this article for the Mail on Sunday on 15 May 2005.

Today the World looks on in horror as scores, perhaps hundreds, of pro-democracy demonstrators in Andizhan pay with their lives the price of Western support for the evil Uzbek dictator, Islam Karimov. George Bush and Tony Blair are culpable in these deaths. They have supported Karimov and obstructed the growth of democratic opposition in the country.

The Uzbek regime has attempted to portray the dissidents as Islamic militants. The White House has been keen to parrot this, saying the demonstrators include 'Islamic terrorists'. This is how they justify continued support to their favourite dictator, and a regime which has literally been known to boil opponents alive. But the charge is simply a lie. Those demonstrating are not Islamic militants. They simply want freedom, democracy and above all a chance to make a living away from the continued Soviet economic system of Uzbekistan.

I know this because I know them. A year ago I traveled to Andizhan as British Ambassador, to attend a meeting of an organisation called the 'Democratic Forum'. This was an attempt to set up an umbrella grouping of supporters of democratic change, with the aim of contesting parliamentary elections held in Uzbekistan last December. At least two of the people at that meeting were among the 23 'Islamic militants' whose imprisonment sparked the current uprising. In fact they were businessmen who wanted capitalism and democracy to come to Uzbekistan.

The Uzbek government tried hard to stop me getting to Andizhan that day. We were stopped at repeated police road blocks, one of which I physically overturned to get past, to the consternation of the Uzbek security services, who couldn't shoot Her Majesty's Ambassador.

We had been followed for miles by a car containing four leather jacketed men. When we stopped for tea they stopped too and sat at the next table. At the last police check point they overtook us. As we entered Andizhan City they emerged at speed from a side street and tried to ram us. Only the brilliance of our Embassy driver, Sasha, saved us from this unfortunate 'Accident'.

I kept up relationships with the Andizhan opposition after my visit. They came to my office several times. Andizhan had been a comparatively wealthy town and its middle class had been particularly hit by government anti-enterprise measures taken from November 2002. Alarmed that slight economic liberalisation was leading to the start of an independently minded middle class, the Uzbek government had clamped down on the private sector. Borders were physically closed to private trade, and in the Ferghana Valley near Andizhan cross-border bridges were dynamited. Bazaars were closed by the security forces. Laws were passed ending cash trading and forcing all business transactions to go through state-owned and controlled banks. The economic effects were catastrophic, especially in a dynamic trading town like Andizhan.

There was no outlet for the resulting discontent. There is absolutely no media freedom in Uzbekistan. The Democratic Forum got nowhere. The opposition were banned from the parliamentary elections, which were farcically contested between five government 'parties' all supporting the President. We are Back in the USSR.

Yet President Karimov, the great oppressor of liberty and capitalism, has the strong support of George Bush. He is a welcome guest for tea in the White House. Donald Rumsfeld, Condoleezza Rice and Colin Powell have all been to Tashkent and lavished praise upon their host. Tony Blair and Jack Straw were all too willing to sack me for speaking out against Karimov's habit of arresting, very often torturing and sometimes killing political opponents.

US Collusion With the Andizhan Massacre

This article attacking White House attempts to cover up the Andizhan massacre was carried by the Guardian on 16 May 2005

The bodies of hundreds of pro-democracy protesters in Uzbekistan are scarcely cold, and already the White House is looking for ways to dismiss them. The White House spokesman Scott McClellan said those shot dead in the city of Andizhan included "Islamic terrorists" offering armed resistance. They should, McClellan insists, seek democratic government "through peaceful means, not through violence".

But how? This is not Georgia, Ukraine or even Kyrgyzstan. There, the opposition parties could fight elections. The results were fixed, but the opportunity to propagate their message brought change. In Uzbek elections on December 26, the opposition was not allowed to take part at all.

And there is no media freedom. On Saturday morning, when Andizhan had been leading world news bulletins for two days, most people in the capital, Tashkent, still had no idea anything was happening. Nor are demonstrations in the capital tolerated. On December 7 a peaceful picket at the gates of the British embassy was broken up with great violence, its victims including women and children. So how can Uzbeks pursue democracy by "peaceful means"?

Take the 23 businessmen whose trial for "Islamic extremism" sparked recent events. Had the crowd not sprung them from jail, what would have awaited them? The conviction rate in criminal and political trials in Uzbekistan is over 99% - in President Karimov's torture chambers, everyone confesses.

But the torture by no means ends on conviction. In prison there is torture to make you sign a recantation of faith and declaration of loyalty to the president. And there is torture to make you sign evidence implicating "accomplices". It was at this stage that the infamous boiling to death of Muzafar Avazov and Husnidin Alimov took place in Jaslik prison in 2002. I expect the government will take care that the 23, if not already dead, die in the mopping up.

You may think I exaggerate. Read the 2002 report by Professor Theo van Boven, the UN special rapporteur on torture, in which he denounced torture in Uzbekistan as "widespread and systemic". Human Rights Watch last year produced a book with more than 300 pages of case studies. One of the uses of Uzbek torture is to provide the CIA and MI6 with "intelligence" material linking the Uzbek opposition with Islamist terrorism and al-Qaida. The information is almost entirely bogus, and it was my efforts to stop MI6 using it that led ultimately to my effective dismissal from the Foreign Office.

The information may be untrue, but it is valuable because it feeds into the US agenda. Karimov is very much George Bush's man in central Asia. There is not a senior member of the US administration who is not on record saying warm words about Karimov. There is not a single word recorded by any of them calling for free elections in Uzbekistan.

And it's not just words. In 2002, the US gave Uzbekistan over $500m in aid, including $120m in military aid and $80m in security aid. The level has declined - but not nearly as much as official figures seem to show (much is hidden in Pentagon budgets after criticism of the 2002 figure).

The airbase opened by the US at Khanabad is not essential to operations in Afghanistan, its claimed raison d'etre. It has a more crucial role as the easternmost of

Donald Rumsfeld's "lily pads" - air bases surrounding the "wider Middle East", by which the Pentagon means the belt of oil and gas fields stretching from the Middle East through the Caucasus and central Asia. A key component of this strategic jigsaw fell into place this spring when US firms were contracted to build a pipeline to bring central Asia's hydrocarbons out through Afghanistan to the Arabian sea. That strategic interest explains the recent signature of the US-Afghan strategic partnership agreement, as well as Bush's strong support for Karimov. So the Uzbek people can keep on dying. They are not worth a lot of cash, so who cares? I traveled to Andizhan a year ago to meet the opposition leaders, and kept in touch. I can give you a direct assurance that they are - or in many cases were - in no sense Islamist militants. They died an unwanted embarrassment to US foreign policy. We will doubtless hear some pious hypocrisies from Jack Straw. But when I was seeking funding to support the proto-democrats, the Foreign Office turned me down flat.

The US will fund "human rights" training in Uzbekistan but not help for the democratic opposition, in contrast to its policy elsewhere in the former Soviet Union. When Jon Purnell, the US ambassador, last year attended the opening of a human rights centre in the Ferghana valley, he interrupted a local speaker criticising repression. Political points, Purnell opined, were not allowed.

The western news agenda has moved the dead of Andizhan from the "democrat" to the "terrorist" pile. Karimov remains in power. The White House will be happy. That's enough for No 10.

60 Second Interview

On 17 May 2005 this interview appeared with The Metro newspaper in their regular "Sixty second" slot.

As Britain's Ambassador to the Central Asian republic of Uzbekistan, Craig Murray spoke out against the human rights abuses of the US-funded regime long before the recent massacre. He lost his job last year and stood against Foreign Secretary Jack Straw in the General Election to protest against Western policy in the region and the war in Iraq.

You warned more than a year ago that Uzbekistan would explode. How angry are you to see it happening?

It gives me no pleasure to be proved right. It's interesting to see the hypocrisy of Jack Straw and others claiming they are doing something. We've long known that this was a terrible regime and it was bound to lead to public protest. And we knew that the regime would act viciously against that protest. President Karimov has the arrogance that comes from knowing he has the support of both Washington and Moscow.

President Karimov of Uzbekistan is a brutal dictator but he's our dictator. Discuss.

Yes, that's very much the American line. They argue that our alliance with Karimov is a necessary evil, like our alliance with Stalin in Word War II. There is no such comparison. The only factor driving radical Islam in Central Asia is people despairing at the regime and the lack of any democratic alternative.

What happens next?

Not much. We'll see more hypocrisy from the US and the UK, calling for everything short of actual change. Democratic elections within a year are the only thing that will defuse the situation. There is no sign we're going to call for that, nor that we're going to stop calling Uzbekistan 'our ally in the war on terror', nor that the US is going to stop giving the regime a few hundred million dollars a year. There's no sign Jack Straw will stop using intelligence from the Uzbek security services which is extracted by torture. Coming out of the torture chambers will be people 'admitting' they were working for Osama Bin Laden, and Washington will give some credence to all that nonsense.

Intelligence produced through torture is bad intelligence. Why are the CIA addicted to it?

Well, it's plainly immoral and illegal. Secondly, it's rubbish. But while the material is untrue, that doesn't mean it's not useful. The US Government is delighted to have material that says the Uzbek opposition are Islamic militants. It gives them the excuse to go on backing Karimov.

Is the 'War on Terror' a genuine threat or a fantasy from the intelligence services?

A great deal of it is a fantasy. The intelligence about weapons of mass destruction wasn't true, either, but it was extremely useful. The same is true of intelligence that allows former Met Police Chief John Stevens to say there are 200 Islamic terrorists active in Britain. Active Islamic terrorists, prepared to sacrifice their own lives, but they haven't managed to kill anyone yet. Not very good terrorists, are they? It's all complete rubbish designed to keep the population in a state of fear. Tanks at Heathrow to keep a suicide bomber off a plane? It's plainly bollocks - hype.

We topple an evil dictator in Iraq, yet support an evil dictator in Uzbekistan. Why the paradox? You can't believe Tony Blair and Jack Straw are evil or stupid.

There certainly are evil people in the White House and the Pentagon. The decision has been taken that, in the war on terror, Britain should be extremely close to the

US. Jack Straw finds the alliance over Uzbekistan distasteful but he's held his nose and got on with it. The Americans are cynical; their interest in Central Asia is all about oil and gas. We back a dictator in Central Asia to get access to oil and gas, and we remove a dictator in Iraq to get access to oil and gas. Explain American policy in terms of freedom and democracy and you get a contradiction. Explain it in terms of oil and gas and it's completely consistent.

Well, the US is the world's greatest economy. It's your business to get rid of anything threatening your fuel supplies. What's wrong with that?

Well, they want to get access to it so they can burn it up as quickly as possible in their massive gas-guzzling cars and with a total lack of concern for energy conservation. They will drive forward global warming.

But they don't believe in global warming...

They claim not to. You have to tie in this political stance to their refusal to sign the Kyoto Agreement. That's what makes it all so bloody disastrous.

To deny the reality sounds stupid, almost insane.

It's not insane to the interests promoting it. They stand to make huge fortunes in oil and gas. It's the energy companies who are the lobbyists for the non-existence of global warming. They are just pursuing a very narrow personal interest, which is typical of America. Often they are stupid and their policy in Uzbekistan is extremely stupid. They are going to create Islamic fundamentalism. But this is all in the interests of the military establishment - a bigger threat means more money, better pay, more jobs etc. I seem to have developed a very cynical world view.

What can a Metro reader do?

Write to their MP. As someone who has worked in the Foreign Office, I can tell you it has much more effect than you might think. The MP passes it on and it has to be answered within a week. Six letters and they think the electorate is fascinated by this subject. Write and demand free elections in Uzbekistan and demand we stop calling it an ally.

Britain's Pusillanimous Diplomacy

Fury at the feeble British official reaction to the Andizhan Massacre seethes throughout this article for the Financial Times on 21 May 2005.

I have lost count of the number of journalists who have asked me 'Do you feel vindicated?' My replies to that one have been unprintable. How can you feel vindicated by several hundred dead people? Mostly I just feel miserable. I think we are in a real sense culpable. It is Western support for Karimov that gives him such arrogant assurance in gunning down his opponents.

Ever since I heard by email about three weeks ago - that street protests were taking off in Andizhan, I had been longing to be there. I would never get a visa, but was speculating about getting over from Kirghizstan on a smuggler's route. Once the massacre happened sections of border were out of control for a few days. I desperately wanted to go. Annoyingly, I have to go into hospital tomorrow for a heart operation on Monday. I have been trying to convince myself that I have done more good by media work here.

That desire to be there did not entail a longing to be British Ambassador again. At least, not until Wednesday, when I saw reports of the pathetic trip by diplomats to inspect the scene. I had predicted on ITN that this would be 'a nauseating propaganda charade'. It was. They traveled in a tightly controlled convoy on a sealed off route. The blood had been hosed away. The government dictated who they could meet. The only civilian was the father of a dead soldier. This charabanc trip ended an hour and a half before they expected ' Karimov doesn't just get the buses to run on time, they even run early. The bulk of the time was taken in a formal banquet.

My successor, David Moran, bleated 'Can we not meet some people?' Of course you can. At that moment I wished I was back in his shoes. You just walk out, pushing past the soldiers, down to the bazaar, and talk to people. One of my more delightful memories was of Clare Short doing exactly that in May 2003, to the huge consternation of the regime. You, David, are one of the tiny number of people in Uzbekistan they can't shoot. No-one physically forced you to spend the bulk of your precious time in Andizhan on your arse.

I have been keeping up with events both from phone and email contacts to Uzbekistan, and via the internet. I see The Australian has reported I had a habit of manhandling obstructive Uzbek officials (how did they know?). I wouldn't call it a habit, but you do sometimes have to show in a totalitarian state that you are not going to be obstructed in your work. To be fair to David Moran, his semi-protest showed at least some backbone; it was more than most of my senior ex-colleagues would have done.

The next day we had the Uzbek Prokurator General announcing that 170 people had, after all, been killed but that they were all armed rebels. I did feel vindicated by the sheer disbelief that greeted this. Here is why.

In March 2004 there were a series of explosions and shootings in Tashkent, in which at least thirty people died. I dashed round to the scene of each incident, arriving within hours or even minutes, accompanied by Giles Whittell of the Times who had just walked in to the Embassy to interview me.

Suicide bombers from the Islamic Movement of Uzbekistan, linked to Al Qaida, had carried out a series of attacks on security forces. That remains the internationally accepted version of events. But it isn't true.

I attended the briefings the Prokurator General gave to

journalists and diplomats. His claims were completely incompatible with the facts I observed. He said suicide belts had been used each with the force of two kilos of TNT. But at the sites there just wasn't the physical damage. Not so much as a cracked paving stone, let alone a crater. The first 'bomb' had been in a roughly triangular courtyard thirty metres wide at maximum. Allegedly six soldiers and a suicide bomber had been killed. Not a pane of glass was broken in the buildings overlooking the courtyard, not a branch or sprig torn from the tree in the centre.

My reports that the Prokurator General was lying through his teeth brought me startled reproof from my management in London. You see, the attacks by Islamic terrorists fitted our narrative. So I feel a personal relief that the lies are at last being exposed.

United States Ejected from Uzbekistan

When the United States was ejected from its Uzbek airbase and other interests in August 2005, the US government tried to portray this as a voluntary withdrawal as a human rights protest. In this Guardian article of 3 August 2005 Craig Murray nailed this lie and noted in fact they had been comprehensively out-maneuvered by Putin over oil deals.

In retrospect, this was the first evidence of Putin's mastery of international relations in his efforts to re-assert Russian influence abroad.

President Karimov of Uzbekistan has served notice to quit on the US base in his country. This completes a process of diplomatic revolution as Karimov turns away from the west and back into the embrace of Russia, with coy sideways glances at China. The US is trying to cover its retreat behind a smokescreen of belated concern for human-rights abuse in Uzbekistan. Suddenly one of their most intensively courted allies has been discovered - shock horror - to be an evil dictator. (Remember Saddam?) But the reality is much more complex.

The first and most obvious point is that the US didn't jump, it was pushed. The Andizhan massacre of May 13, in which at least 600 demonstrators were killed, was carried out by Uzbek forces that in 2002 alone received $120m in US aid for the army and $82m for the security services. Prior to Karimov kicking it out, there was no indication at all that the US was going to review its military links with Uzbekistan - in fact General Richard Myers had specifically stated that they would continue.

In March this year the British army sent a team to Samarkand to teach the Uzbek military marksmanship.

We have not said we will stop either. Nor has there been any indication that we will stop the practice whereby the Uzbek security services share with the CIA and MI6 the so-called intelligence extracted from Karimov's torture chambers. So much for the pretence of moral repugnance.

At Termez in southern Uzbekistan there is another, less noticed, western airbase. It is leased by Germany. The Germans are not seeking to withdraw. Of all western ministers, the most frequent guest in Uzbekistan, who most uncritically praises the regime, is Joschka Fischer, the trendy German foreign minister.

The EU general affairs council, chaired by Jack Straw, responded to the Andizhan massacre by announcing that it would, for a short time, "suspend further deepening" of the EU-Uzbek cooperation agreement. I can recognise FCO drafting when I see it - such an elegant phrase. You have to read it twice to realise that it precisely means "do nothing".

Karimov has never intended to move Uzbekistan towards democracy or the free market. His very limited experimentation with attracting western investment in the mid-1990s convinced him that western-style capitalism was incompatible with containing all economic clout in the hands of his family and immediate cronies. Since then he has turned to Russian and Chinese state companies for investment.

The writing was really on the wall for US influence in central Asia when, at the end of last year, Karimov finally came off the fence and opted for Russia's Gazprom rather than US firms to develop Uzbekistan's massive gas fields. The decision calls into question the viability of the hydrocarbons pipeline over Afghanistan to the Arabian Sea, which has been the holy grail of US policy in central Asia since before the Afghan war. The deal was concluded between Karimov's notoriously grasping daughter, Gulnara Karimova, and Alisher Usmanov, the Uzbek-born Russian oligarch who bought heavily into Corus (formed by the merger of British Steel and the Dutch company Hoogovens in 1999).

Many believe that a Karimova-Usmanov alliance is Karimov's preferred succession strategy. But certainly Moscow resident Gulnara has had a vital influence on the reorientation of Uzbek foreign policy. She cannot enter the US, where there is a warrant for her arrest for contempt of court following a disputed divorce case.

The other key factor has been the "colour revolutions" in Ukraine, Georgia and Kyrgyzstan. Eduard Shevardnadze visited Karimov on being ousted and warned him against Soros and other NGOs. Karimov immediately kicked out the Open Society Institute and put crippling restrictions on other NGOs, setting his face against even token democracy. This helped the increasingly warm relationship with Vladimir Putin.

Karimov was, on the face of it, an unlikely man for Putin to embrace. After independence he had encouraged anti-Russian nationalist sentiment, and 80% of ethnic Russians - more than 2 million people - fled Uzbekistan.

But Putin and Karimov have in common an intolerance of opposition, a contempt for free media, and a desire to stem the spread of democracy. Karimov's policy of brutally eliminating opponents while accusing them all of Islamic extremism has obvious parallels with Putin's policy in Chechnya.

Where does this leave the regional power game? Uzbekistan has half the population of central Asia, a dominant geo-strategic position and the region's largest and best-equipped armed forces. But to the north, Kazakhstan, under President Nazarbayev, has far outstripped Karimov in economic performance, and not only because of greater hydrocarbon resources. He has kept a balance between Russia and the west, and the economy is relatively open, with much more western investment.

The future of Kazakhstan looks relatively bright. In fact one of the key factors in Karimov's soaring unpopularity is that Kazakhs, once despised poor cousins, are now much wealthier.

But the prospects for Kyrgyzstan and Tajikistan are bleak. They are tiny, mountainous countries with few viable natural resources. The US still has a viable airbase in Kyrgyzstan. Karimov, backed by Russia and China in the Shanghai cooperation council, is likely to exert massive pressure on them to also turn away from the west. If they are to be able to resist this, a huge effort will be required by western countries and international agencies.

So what happens now in Uzbekistan? As the world's powers wheel and spin, the plight of the Uzbek population deepens. Karimov's appalling policies keep his people in ever-greater poverty, effectively a slave-labour force working, most of them on state farms, for the enrichment of his family and cronies. The economy is heavily dependent on massive production of cotton, the revenue from which brings almost no economic benefit to the wretches who pick it in conditions of serfdom.

We should be seeking to shorten Uzbekistan's misery, not to extend it. It is the world's second largest exporter of cotton. Citing the use of child and serf labour, concerted trade sanctions against Uzbek cotton and textiles containing Uzbek cotton should be the way forward. Given the self-interest of the very powerful US cotton lobby and the new frost in US-Uzbek relations, this might even be achievable.

British Embassy Abandons Human Rights Role in Uzbekistan

Receiving this letter from Uzbekistan on 4 May 2007 caused Craig Murray considerable emotional distress.

Just after blogging yesterday that I had received 317 emails from people who had read "Murder in Samarkand", I received the 318th. This one is unusual in that it is from someone I know slightly, an Uzbek I tried to help four years ago. I publish it because I think it is important, not least in what it says about the British Embassy in Tashkent no longer helping the oppressed. I have removed all details that may help the Uzbek government identify the sender.

> Dear Mr Murray,
> My name is... I wonder if you still remember me. I met you in Uzbekistan in ... I was Uzbek student who studied ... I remember I came to you desperately seeking for help from aggressive and abusive actions of Uzbek police and you helped me that time. You even went to police station with me trying to protect me from possible physical abuse. ... I can not speak against Uzbek authorities because my relatives and friends are in Uzbekistan and they have been threatened by bloody SNB, that they all would have a huge problems if I am going to act like a decedent.
> So, since then I am keeping myself quite, keeping all of the anger inside me. Here I met Andizhan tragedy, and other abusive and terrible actions of Uzbek terrorist government. Would you believe or not I did not even have any contacts with Uzbek people in ... I distanced myself from everything linked with Uzbekistan.
> And then I bought your book and memorable emotions filled my head. I read whole your book in just 2 days.

Every time I turned pages tears were on my eyes. Everything came to my memory, my childhood, my university ages, my friends, my parents and then my problems. I remembered neighbourhood where I lived in ... gathering with my friends. It is terrible what regime did to people. At least I am alive and live in ... dream for many Uzbek people. I did not know, that regime was behaving so badly with foreign diplomats as well. I thought only Uzbeks deserved such brutal behaviour. I knew, that you were brave person, but when I read your book, I could not believe how much brave you are. You did more for Uzbek people than any Uzbek ever did. You gave us hope, that regime is not something which has unlimited power, that people can strike against this terrible persons.

After you have been sacked, British Embassy is not a place for desperate people anymore. Nobody cares about torture. Embassy became the same place it was before you. Of course after your experience nobody will want to have the same troubles with FCO. Now they are paying the price. Labours' rating is the lowest as it ever was. They betrayed the person who really did a lot to increase British prestige among the most of Uzbek people. There were even uneducated people who knew there is some place in Tashkent where they can find a protection, where they at least can be listened. So it was, but it worse now. NGOs have been closed, talented students do not have chance to study abroad anymore, instead they should study BLOODY Karimov's books, this lie, this hypocrisy.

Thinking about all of these, I do not regret that I left Uzbekistan, even those, I live here alone without any relatives or friends. I regret only about how mane more people will become victims of this terrible, brutal, inhuman regime. How many more people should suffer, or being killed before this BUSTARD Karimov and his BLOODY dogs will go. I spoke with some people here about this, but nobody knows. One thing is certain, that it can not last forever. My situation is much better now. I have more or less good job, probably the best that immigrant refugee can get.... I am working as ....

I just dream, that one day we, I mean Uzbeks, can live free without being threatened. But, I do not know when, and how to make these days happened. I have spoken with ...by the way big hello to you from him, and he told me that it would be very bloody way to get rid of regime. This conversation was even before Andizhan tragedy, and history proved his opinion. He also was terrified after Andizhan and said that it was too much blood for nothing.

I do not know if you were drinking alcohol, or having sex with women, but one thing is certain, is that you were the best diplomat UK could ever have. You cared about Human values of freedom and life, and cared about foreign non-British people when you saw, what a disaster is around them. You were doing the same things UK and US governments were talking about before Iraq invasion, that they were going to protect Iraqis from tyranny and gave them freedom. But instead that sacked their diplomat who was trying to implement this programme. What a hypocrisy.

I am sorry for my long letter, full of emotions. Two years I tried to forget about all of these and then suddenly bought your book and remembered everything.

I live in .. will be one day and will...wish to meet, I would be very happy. It will be very big honour for me to meet with you. Thank you very much for everything you did and still doing for Uzbek people and for me personally.

Our Man in Blackburn

Craig Murray decided to take on Jack Straw by standing against him as an independent candidate in the 2005 general election, despite never having been to Blackburn before. His remarkable campaign attracted volunteers from around the globe. In the end he secured precisely 5% of the vote.

He chronicled his campaign experience in these weekly articles for the Guardian newspaper, beginning on 17 March 2005. The Guardian heavily edited these articles; what follows are the original drafts.

The idea of my standing against Jack Straw in Blackburn at the general election had been born in conversation with Andrew Gilligan, when he was interviewing me for the Channel 4 Documentary Torture - the Dirty Business shown last Tuesday.

I had been talking about Jack Straw's role in approving the use by MI6 of information obtained under torture by the Uzbek security services. Gilligan's film had shown that the same was happening in Egypt, Syria and elsewhere, and that the CIA were kidnapping terrorist suspects around the globe and shipping them to places where they could be tortured.

I have the advantage of having seen some of the so-called intelligence this process produces, and know it to be nonsense aimed at exaggerating the role, strength and links of Al-Qaida and Bin Laden. Yet the government wishes to be able, on the meagre strength of such intelligence, to keep people detained or under house arrest indefinitely, without access to fair trial.

Both Clark and Blair smugly cite "intelligence" as though it were some infallible source of information to which only the trustworthy few - ie them - have access.

In fact this intelligence is dead dodgy, about as reliable as a racing tip from a bent jockey. If you don't want to take my word for it, consider the dossier of lies on Iraqi Weapons of Mass Destruction.

Anyway, Gilligan and I were discussing how to hold Straw accountable for his decision on torture material, for the WMD dossier (he is, after all, in charge of MI6, a fact Hutton almost failed to notice), and for the illegal war on Iraq. This is meant to be a democracy, I mused. Why not challenge him at the polls, in his own backyard? I boldly declared I would go ahead and challenge Straw. News of it spread, and I found I had somehow passed a point of no return. It had to be done.

I hope to give Straw a run for his money in Blackburn. But still more, I hope that I will be able to keep the media focus on the torture, human rights and illegal war. This is of course precisely what Blair doesn't want. "Let's move on from that" is his mantra.

Am I the only one to find this insulting? I think I'll rob a bank to fund my election campaign. When the police come to arrest me, I shall say: "Hey, let's move on from that. OK I robbed a bank, but that was last week. You should see my great plans for the future. I realise that robbing the bank may have raised some trust issues, but I think if you will really listen to me we can establish a dialogue and overcome those."

Anyway it was now time to translate my resolve into action on the ground. After a day of London media interviews, at seven o clock in the evening I set out from Shepherd's Bush in a freezing, driving rain for a preparatory visit to my prospective constituents.

The first part of the trip was in a Virgin Pendalino train. I can't say I noticed it tilting, but it got me to Manchester fast, comfortably and efficiently. Two more changes of train saw me arriving in Blackburn just on midnight on a local service. It was a bitterly cold night with sharp specks of snow. The local train had no heating system and reminded me of a Polish tram of the communist era.

I had not booked a hotel, figuring that Blackburn was the sort of place that would be bound to have a big old Victorian station hotel. I had visions of a large bed, velvet curtains and piping hot cast iron radiators. Well it did, but it shut. There were several vans of very cold looking policemen at the railway station, for no apparent reason. I asked one where I might find a hotel, and he replied, cryptically: "You'll be lucky."

After a frozen plod through the snow, I came to a minicab firm, and a very chirpy driver called Ajit bundled me into his people carrier. He explained that the Blackburn Rovers vs Burnley FA Cup 5th Round replay had just finished. The two being neighbours and bitter rivals, the game was the biggest event in Blackburn for a long time. The hotels would be full with supporters, he opined.

I had known the game was on, but told Ajit that Burnley being just down the road, I had not expected the hotels would be affected. He said that the hotels were full not of Burnley but of Blackburn supporters; they came from all over for matches. I presume this is a Blackburn diaspora; in England it is only at Old Trafford that the majority of so-called fans have no connection to the local population.

Anyway, Ajit was sure that the Travel Inn would have rooms. It didn't, but then he was sure that the Travel Lodge would have rooms. After that we tried the Fernhurst, the Bear, the Woodlands, the Hilltop and a couple of others. Not the Chimneys though - Ajit warned me they were rum folk at the Chimneys.

Ajit remained continually cheerful and optimistic, and I am quite sure he didn't deliberately keep ferrying across town in a series of five mile swings, but soon it was 1.30am there was £40 on the clock and still nowhere to sleep. Ajit had suggested trying outside Blackburn, but I was loathe to go scuttling ignominiously away at the start of my first visit. Finally, however, I had to admit defeat and we took a brief trip down the motorway to the Preston Novotel. It was an inauspicious start to my Blackburn campaign; there was no room at the inn.

The next morning I took a taxi into town and stood outside Blackburn Cathedral clutching my bag, my hands turning blue with cold. I headed into the visitor centre to get a coffee, and bumped into a documentary crew making a film about MPAC, the Muslim Public Affairs Committee. They had filmed me last week meeting MPAC to discuss the Blackburn campaign, so we greeted each other. I sat down to drink my coffee, and they filmed me doing it.

Revived, I went out to scout around for a vacant shop I could rent as an HQ for three months. There were several suitable looking empty shops available. I also called on letting agents to find somewhere to live for three months, but they all said the minimum let was six months.

All the shops to let seemed to use the same agent, Trevor Dawson. I telephoned this company and explained what I wanted and why. They replied rather cryptically that commercial property owners in Blackburn would not want to be associated with any campaign against Jack Straw. Nonetheless I asked them to check the availability of two shops which particularly interested me.

I bought a local newspaper; I saw a Blackburn labour councillor had just been convicted of vote rigging, and been told by the judge to expect a custodial sentence. The rigging had been using postal ballots among the Muslim community.

Blackburn's Muslim community is primarily Gujerati, and has traditionally been a bulwark of Straw's support. By chance, Jack Straw went on an official visit to Gujerat only last week, where he made much of Home Office proposals to make it easier to get visas to visit relatives (I'll believe that when I see it). The Mail on Sunday was distasteful enough to suggest that this pre-election visit was electioneering at public expense.

The host authorities have said that the initiative to visit Gujerat specifically came from the British side. I have put in a request to the FCO under the Freedom of Information Act for papers relating to the genesis of this visit; doubtless these will clear Jack's name of any electioneering purpose.

Straw is a master of Labour machine politics and of the use of patronage; he has made two patriarchs of his constituency Gujerati community members of the House of Lords. One of Lord Patel's daughters has a well paid job on the board of the local NHS Trust; the rumour in the pubs of Blackburn is that she has only turned up twice.

There is much speculation that the War on Terror will turn the Muslim vote against Straw, but the ennobled leadership remains firmly behind him. There is a thought that disillusioned young Muslims might split from the leadership, but this is where the postal ballot comes in.

The great disadvantage of the secret ballot is that, whatever social pressure you may have exerted, you have no idea what the individual does in the ballot box. This is where Labour's innovation of widespread postal voting is so helpful to them. Community patriarchs can insist on inspecting the ballots before voting, something they couldn't do in the polling station. Or they can even collect up all the postal ballots and fill them in themselves, which is precisely what the Blackburn Labour councillor was convicted of.

It is going to be very interesting to watch what happens with postal ballots in this election in Blackburn certainly, but elsewhere as well. I for one am deeply suspicious of Blair's enthusiasm for them.

At lunchtime I am surprised by a phone call from a television crew from the Australian Broadcasting Corporation. They are at Blackburn station. They are making a documentary about me, but I thought I had given them the slip. Evidently not, and for the rest of the day the citizens of Blackburn are mildly surprised by the sight of me wandering round in the snow being filmed by a bunch of Australians, who seem particularly keen on repeated shots of me walking purposefully and gazing nobly into the distance.

Before going on to an interview with Radio Lancashire, I do one with the Australian correspondent, Evan Williams. We take off our coats and are seated on a bench outside the cathedral; small spears of ice are sweeping horizontally into my face. I struggle against the cold and wind to explain why I'm standing in Blackburn. Goodness knows what Australian audiences will think of this: "Here's some pommie nutter sitting in a churchyard in a blizzard. Must be a reality TV endurance show."

The Australians follow me in to Radio Lancashire, filming away. I am interviewed by Chris Ryder, who is relentlessly hostile. He starts off by saying "Are you standing against Jack Straw just because he sacked you". Questions include "You do realise that Jack Straw's an extremely popular constituency MP?"

I immediately concede I have no local background, and as yet very little knowledge of Blackburn, but he still ploughs through a dozen questions aimed at hammering this home. I make my points about torture, intelligence, house arrest, and illegal war. He doesn't respond to anything I say. He is reading from a list of questions and doesn't deviate from them, whatever I am saying. I wonder where they were prepared. The interview is pre-recorded, although I had requested live. I wonder how many of my more telling points will actually get broadcast.

As we leave I give the Australians - who are still filming - a wry grin. "Jeez, what a wanker" says Evan. I hope they leave that bit in. Come to think of it, I hope the Guardian leave it in too.

In the evening I do a tour of the pubs. Blackburn is blessed with excellent beer from the big Thwaites brewery, still family owned. Thwaites cask beer is a real classic. Blackburn also has a micro brewery, 3Bs. This produces some really good beers, including a mild, Stoker's Slake, full of burnt and caramelly flavours and a potent reminder of how much we are losing as this style of beer becomes increasingly rare.

I have managed to get a room at the Fernhurst Hotel - also owned by Thwaites - and finally get to sleep in my chosen constituency.

The next morning brings good news. The two shops I specified are both available. They both belong to Thwaites. I choose the one on Lower Church Street, behind the vast modern shopping centre. It has two pubs to its immediate right and one to its left. Only one of these three - the Sun - is working.

That is one of Blackburn's most striking features. It has an astonishing number of ex-pubs. Some have been converted to other uses, but many more are derelict. Blackburn has closed more pubs than other cities had in the first place. I wonder why there were so many and what factors caused this cull. Something else I have yet to learn.

I meet an old acquaintance from University, Stuart, who is a former Blackburn Tory councillor and also a printer. We go to his offices in India Mill, a cathedral to manufacturing vacated by Coates Viyella when the British textile industry collapsed in the eighties. It has a great chimney styled as a Venetian campanile - I remember watching Fred Dibnah climb it on TV. From Stuart's windows you can look out on the great Crown wallpaper factory, closed three years ago. We design posters and leaflets.

I feel the campaign is really getting underway. I go to the local newspaper offices and give an interview to a thoughtful young reporter named Caroline. She looks to have forty years less experience of journalism than Chris Ryder; forty years less narrowing of the mind. Then it's parading up and down outside the cathedral again, while the local paper take photographs.

I put in a classified ad for a house to rent. Then I go off to meet some Asian community leaders, who seem pretty enthused before boarding a train to Chesterfield. There I am a guest speaker at the Green Party conference. I am on good emotional form and get a very enthusiastic standing ovation when I finish. I feel things are going well.

Back in London I have messages waiting for me to call Martin Bell and Brian Eno. I do so, and both want to help my campaign. The warm glow of this is quickly dissipated by news from the Estate Agent. Thwaites Brewery have decided they will not let me rent any of their property in Blackburn. Their estates manager had been overruled by directors who felt it would not be in the company's interests to allow their premises to be used to campaign against Jack Straw.

This causes me to re-assess soberly what I had achieved on my first showing in Blackburn. Not much. And while my emails are full of offers from talented people to write copy, handle media and design the website, I still have nothing solid in place locally.

Next week I will be conducting the Blackburn campaign from the Austrian Institute of International Affairs, who have asked me to lecture in Vienna. As the phoney general election breaks into real hostilities, this campaign diary will become increasingly frequent.

*****

The sun is shining in Blackburn and spirits are light. Well, mine are. I am sitting in my new campaign headquarters. My assistants are Peter Newton and Eddie Duxbury, two pensioners. Pete is cleaning the windows and Eddie is setting up the computers and telephones. I managed to rent a shop in a perfect town-centre position, just down from the railway centre.

Campaigning is going well. I am enjoying my encounters with the voters, who are given to speaking their minds. I have met with no hostility. I have been invited for cups of tea by total strangers. One thing that has surprised me when I have gone leafleting is that it is not unusual for people to leave their front doors ajar. On some streets, children run about and play football in the road as I did as a child. These are things London has lost.

As I walk around with my sack of leaflets, I appreciate that Blackburn is pretty hilly. There are a lot of low-density, prosperous-looking new housing estates. In one of them yesterday it took me nearly three hours to deliver 120 leaflets. But there are also many areas of terraced houses with front doors that open on to the pavement - a leafleter's dream. On Balaclava and Inkerman streets, I did 120 leaflets in 20 minutes: battery voters.

To be fair, Jack Straw is an assiduous constituency MP. I had presumed that would mean he is a popular one, but apparently not. This is partly because of the war in Iraq. The idea that voters don't care about foreign policy is simply wrong. But there is also a lot of ill-feeling towards the local Labour council. Blackburn has been Labour since 1945. The council is the largest employer in the constituency and has been the channel for huge volumes of urban regeneration funds, much of it from the EU. In short, the council is controlled by one party and controls much of the economy.

Pete and Eddie were office-holders of the Bank Top community association. They became concerned about what had happened to a large sum of urban-regeneration funds earmarked for their community. The council said the funds had been disbursed, but they could not see it on the ground. They started to write inquiring letters.

The council reacted swiftly. It accused them of mismanagement of the very small funds of the community association and removed them from their (unpaid) positions. They appealed to the local government ombudsman, who said the council had the power to act in this way. Perhaps it does; but it left two pensioners humiliated and stigmatised. And they still don't know where the million quid went. It is a fact of life - a local council dominated long term by one party becomes arrogant and cliquish.

I now move on to ground where angels fear to tread. Blackburn is close to the BNP heartlands; the party polled significantly here in the European parliament elections, and the conditions seem to offer potential for the disease to spread. The Muslim population is very segregated; Blackburn has sharply defined Asian and white areas. White people of all ages and political persuasions, including lifelong socialists, complain to me that the massive influx of public money for urban regeneration has benefited almost exclusively the Asian areas. As far as I can judge, this is not a false perception. There may be good reasons for it - presumably the Asian parts of town scored highly on deprivation indices. But people believe it to be connected to the ability of Muslim community leaders to mobilise a massive Labour vote. The resulting perception of unfairness is a real problem, exacerbated by the fact that the Asian community is, on the whole, more upwardly mobile. The schools with largely Asian populations are doing better. Part of the solution must be that more public funds need to be found to equalise provision of community facilities. That will reinforce a dependency culture that already worries me.

Last Friday, I met Muslims outside a Blackburn mosque. Several recognised me and we had a lively conversation about the war and the impact on civil rights. One has a friend imprisoned under the Terrorism Act and wanted me to help. They were welcoming, gentle and curious. Yet the tabloid press could slap any one of them, with their long beards and white skull caps, on the front page with a caption about "Osama's Lieutenant". Muslims are being demonised by a media that is converting their very image into an object of hate. I worry deeply about where this country is heading.

*****

Our campaign is pretty well on the move now, except for continuing telecom problems. It is 10 days since I applied to BT for landlines for our campaign HQ. They called yesterday to tell me an engineer will be available on April 7. I spent much of the day fuming hopelessly at various BT officials, but still no line.

I buy, at great expense, an Orange mobile office card to try to solve my internet problem in the meantime. Rather than wait for pages to download, it would be quicker to travel to the addresses of the websites and ask for a paper copy. I make more irate calls. Orange blames overload on the network, as opposed to its network being no good. It would function perfectly if nobody used it.

We had a minor drama on Maundy Thursday. Our campaign HQ used to be the borough council's information office. They moved out in November, leaving their sign above the premises. It had grown very mucky, but was still legible. The windows are now full of anti-war and anti-Straw posters. The council woke up to this matter the day before the Easter break.

Two officials stood outside looking important and making calls on their mobile phones. Then they asked me to take the sign down, to which I replied: "It's your sign."

An Ealing comedy ensued with lots of people arriving, looking at the sign, and speaking to me. A man from Capita told me that the council had instructed them that the sign must be down that day, before the Easter holiday. After the flood of officials, two painters arrived, having been pulled off work on housing. They proceeded to take down the sign, and I made them a cup of tea. They promised to vote for me.

Capita is an interesting privatised body. It seems to do public works less efficiently than the government used to, and with the senior management getting paid huge amounts of cash - so much that Capita's chief executive is sponsoring a city academy for Blackburn.

This is the government's wonderful new scheme. If you put in less than 10% of the capital cost of the new school, you can have it named after you, and you get a big say in choosing the staff and the curriculum. In the north-east these schools are actually teaching creationism - which, of course, pleases the spooky-eyed religious types on the Blair/Bush axis. Goodness knows what the one in Blackburn will teach. That the Iraq war was legal?

Blackburn is getting a new hospital under the private finance initiative. It seems to me incredible that it can be argued that providing a cash return on capital to the private sector works out cheaper than not doing so. In practice, the result in Blackburn as elsewhere is that the levels of service and facility provision continually dwindle as the project progresses. Can anyone explain to me why we could find ?4bn at the drop of a hat for the war in Iraq, but not public money for a hospital in

Blackburn?

The campaign slog continues. On Monday my girlfriend and I leafleted 1,300 houses between us. My pedometer registered 27 miles, much of it up and down steps. Not wanting to ruin good shoes, I bought a pair in Vienna last month for ?20. They are made of good leather, but have a most unfortunate two-tone effect. A family member told me they make me look like a Russian pimp. I had seen that danger, but rather hoped the effect might be confined to my feet. I can imagine Silvio Berlusconi saying that at a cabinet meeting: "Bring me the feet of that Russian pimp."

There is a real flaw in our democracy, with the odds heavily stacked against independent candidates. On the ballot paper, thanks to a wonderful bit of New Labour Orwellianism, you can no longer choose how to describe yourself. A description such as "Save Kidderminster Hospital" or "No to George Bush" would remind voters of what you stand for. But now you are allowed only to enter the name of a registered political party or the word "Independent".

In each constituency there are strict limits on what you can spend, but no limit on what the parties can spend nationally. So Blackburn hoardings are all plastered with Labour party advertising, which doesn't count against Jack Straw's limit, but any I put up will count against mine. On top of which, fly-posting has been made a specific offence. Well, I think civil disobedience in the name of democracy is called for here. I am off to fly-post Blackburn's many boarded-up buildings.

*****

I obviously haven't got the hang of electoral politics yet. I keep meeting people and hoping they're not going to vote for me. I was watching Jack Straw give one of his soap box orations outside Marks and Spencers when the man standing next to me turned and said 'He's talking rubbish, isn't he'. I agreed, genuinely. 'And you can tell he's Jewish' he added, 'Look at his bloody nose.'

I argued but he wasn't listening. 'I'm not voting for him, anyway', he said; 'I'm voting for that Craig Murray'. I tried to persuade him not to, though I don't think I got through to him who I was. This politics stuff is pretty confusing.

Luckily I have a witness to this next incident, or you wouldn't believe it. I was being interviewed by Deborah Haynes of AFP, a journalist so beautiful I have only just recovered the power to breathe normally. As she was interviewing me, two old ladies came in. They looked like saintlier versions of the Queen Mum, with their white hair, twin sets and handbags.

Ada was 82 and Mabel 83. They had come to offer their support. My gratitude suddenly froze. 'That Jack Straw, his wife's a Paki' said Mabel. Ada backed her up. 'She wears a lot of makeup and keeps her face covered. But I once saw her hand, sticking out of her sleeve'. Ada managed to say this as if sticking out of a sleeve was a particularly sinister place to find a hand. 'And', Ada concluded triumphantly, 'Her hand were black'.

Mabel than added that she intended to go buy a hammer and kill all the Pakis with it.

I had thought that I had lived an unusually full and varied life, but nothing had prepared me for the sight of these two grannies full of hate. I asked them why. The results were interesting. The immediate grievance was that Mabel's Asian neighbour had built a massive home extension, blocking the sunlight from Mabel's garden, which was her pride and joy. The workmen building the extension, which came right to the boundary, had trampled and destroyed it, leaving it strewn with concrete and rubble.

They had been to the Council to complain and discovered that there was no planning permission; but,

Mabel alleged, the neighbour's father was a 'Big man at the mosque' so the Council had done nothing.

Probing further the story gets more interesting. The neighbour the other side of the new extension, a Mr Khan, had also had his garden destroyed and had complained to the Council, without avail.

'So you like Mr Khan.?'

'Oh, yes, Mr Khan's a real gentleman, very polite.'

'And he's Asian?'

Mabel conceded this, reluctantly. I suggested that the problem was not the colour of people's skin, but this was a question of rich, influential people trampling on the rights of the poor and vulnerable. The challenge to their way of thinking was too much for Mabel and Ada, who left. 'We're still buying that hammer' said Ada.

Race relations in Blackburn are at worst dreadful and at best non-existent. I have yet to see a single mixed race social group just chatting together on the street. People work together and transact business, but they don't mix. I met a pleasant lady of Tanzanian origin who told me she has white friends and Asian friends, but not together. Both sides say to her 'You don't mix with them do you?'

The big story of this election is vote-rigging. A Blackburn councillor was last week jailed for three and a half years for vote-rigging in the council elections. There are an astonishing 16,000 postal votes registered in Blackburn, and still rising by two hundred a day. One feature of this fraud mechanism I find most sinister. Postal ballots are mixed in with other ballots before they are counted, so there is no way you can tell if it is rigged. If one candidate loses the main ballot but gets in on eighty per cent of the postal ballot, there is no way you could know. I strongly suspect this might happen in Blackburn now.

I have had, to date, nine people come separately to see

me, all from the Asian community, to complain about intimidation in the current election. One shopkeeper told me that he had been visited by the local Labour councillor who had demanded that all eight of his family must apply for postal ballots, and must show them to the councillor before they are posted. In a rotten borough like Blackburn the council can do a lot of harm to a small shopkeeper.

The Green Goddess is up and running as my campaign bus. It is an alarming vehicle. We have it plastered in posters and going round town blasting out our campaign song 'Hit the road Jack Straw' by The Rub. Martin Bell took a ride in it and declared it scarier than anything he had done as a war reporter.

Martin did a campaign launch for us. About ninety people attended, which for an election meeting nowadays is quite good. The local paper said fifty, and devoted three times as much space to Jack Straw's refutation than to what I said. Some nuts are tougher to crack than others. But I am now ready to make a prediction; Jack Straw's vote will be down to 15,000. He is looking very beatable.

*****

I could actually win this election. The realisation came as something of a shock. It was not really part of the original game plan. Two months ago I arrived here alone, standing forlornly with my rucksack on Blackburn railway station, in the midnight snow. I wanted to make a stand on principle against illegal war, and against Jack Straw's decision that we should use intelligence obtained under torture. I wanted to get some national publicity for these issues during the campaign, to counter Tony Blair's mantra: "Let's move on" from the war.

(Am I the only one to find this mantra insulting? I think I'll rob a bank to get some campaign funds. When the police come to take me away, I'll say, "Hey, let's move on. OK, so I robbed a bank. Whatever the rights and wrongs, that phase is over. What is important is that we all come together now and get behind the really great things I'm going to do with the money.")

Today, however, the campaign HQ is buzzing. Sixty-two local people have so far delivered leaflets for us, in many cases just to their own street. Last night nine volunteers from London were on spare beds and sofas, and 11 more are coming at the weekend. Last weekend, the flood of volunteers included Poles, Ghanaians, Swedes, Canadians and Kiwis.

The Green Goddess is about to go out on yet another mission with a leafleting crew. It is a great campaigning vehicle - a huge free mobile billboard with a big crew cab. It blasts out our campaign song, Hit the Road, Jack Straw by The Rub. The lyrics are really funky: "Yeah, shout out to Blackburn from the rest from the rest of the country/We're hopin' the people in that fine constituency/Can see the new world order ain't no good for humanity./ So hit the road, Jack Straw, and don't you come back no more, no more, no more, no more ... "

The campaign is not popular with everyone. One irate voter called me a middle-class hippy. I was pretty chuffed, having aspired to membership of both for years. I also had an argument with yet another council flunky. This one told me I couldn't park the Goddess outside the town hall to campaign around the shopping centre. I pointed out that Jack Straw regularly does just that. The notion of democracy still seems difficult for some of the authorities here to grasp.

I did some canvassing around the gay bars which are centred, wonderfully, on Mincing Lane. An enthusiastic young man called Geoff told me I was "almost a gay icon, which is really impressive, seeing how you're ugly". Put that on my stone when I go: "Craig Murray. Middle-class hippy. Almost a gay icon."

Robin Cook came to Blackburn to support Jack Straw this week, presumably in a desperate effort to get a place in Gordon Brown's eventual cabinet. Deeply sad. Cook spoke to a strictly limited audience of around 60. The BBC were not admitted, but the Guardian were, up for the day alongside the Murdoch press for a piece on Jack. They accompanied him on a tour that featured carefully staged spontaneity. The everyday activity stumbled across included interracial street football. One local Asian, Vaz, told me he had not seen this in 30 years.

Massoud had let his Labour party membership lapse because of the war. The local party plainly didn't notice, because he was rung and told to be shopping in Asda during Straw's hack-accompanied walkabout. Perhaps that was what Labour offered Asda as an incentive to let them do it - extra shoppers on a Monday morning.

Next week we are anticipating an even stranger source of support for Jack. Local rumour has it that the Saudi ambassador, representative of that fine democracy with a great human rights record, is coming to Blackburn. He and Straw, it seems, will address a meeting of Muslims hosted by the Lancashire Council of Mosques, chairman one Ibrahim Masters, a major Labour party fixer in Blackburn. Announcements are expected of Saudi largesse for the community. Election interference? Perish the thought.

The man who called me a middle-class hippy gave me a note saying, "Don't forget our dead troops." I can't. Much more poignantly, neither can Reg Keays or Rose Gentle. That's why we are standing.

*****

St George's Day is a big thing in Blackburn. England flags sprout from all the shops, and there is a small fair in the town centre, with knights on horseback and a rather cuddly dragon getting slain. Red roses are distributed from a brewer's dray. The Labour party in Blackburn is a rather more fearsome adversary. I noted with some amusement that the main road into town is the A666 - the number of the Beast. Let's hope St George is a good omen.

Politics is banned in the town centre, which on balance is probably OK as it avoids the danger of a BNP takeover of this Englandfest. But it does disappoint a crowd of media people which has gathered in anticipation of Jack Straw and I on rival soapboxes. Maybe next Saturday.

Jack sets up his stall by the rotunda on the other side of the shopping centre. Some of my supporters get the Green Goddess into the multi-storey car park just above his head and start blasting out "Hit the Road Jack Straw". I am down by Jack, doing a Channel 4 interview and, by an acoustic fluke, the sound seems to come from the ground all around us. Great consternation ensues; Labour party hacks bark into mobile phones, and two policemen come running.

The shopping centre security staff eventually find the Green Goddess, climb in and start ripping out the speaker equipment. Some argy-bargy with my team ensues, but eventually it all dusts down quietly.

I have mixed feelings about this kind of thing. A little bit is a good joke, but I don't really approve of trying to drown someone out. On Sunday many of my team go off again to picket a Straw meeting at Jan's conference centre. They enjoy the yelling and venting of fury. I tend to the view that Jack is entitled to run his campaign, but most of my people think he's a war criminal and not entitled to anything but a small cell.

The media circus is getting overwhelming. I have done 11 interviews this morning. But we seem to be blacked by the BBC. On Monday the Ten O'Clock news carried a constituency profile on Blackburn which interviewed the three major party candidates but ignored me. The last mention I had on the BBC was Newsnight a fortnight ago, when Jeremy Paxman read out a highly tendentious statement from the FCO "correcting" a report on the circumstances in which I left my post - something I had not commented on in the first place.

Two days ago someone from Radio 2 called and rather tersely canceled a Simon Mayo interview. Then Radio 5 Live called about a candidates' debate from Blackburn tomorrow. I was now not to participate in the one-hour debate, but was offered an interview of up to five minutes beforehand. I declined.

The Newsnight "correction" had come from FCO civil servants. Clearly, the BBC has been under some pressure. I sent an email to Helen Boaden, head of BBC News and Current Affairs, and asked whether there had been a central decision to downgrade coverage of our campaign, or if these were all programme-producer decisions. I received a reply referring me to the public complaints department.

Meanwhile the campaign goes on. We have now delivered more than 60,000 leaflets to homes in Blackburn. I now feel strongly on one issue: I would support a refusal by postmen to deliver mail to postboxes two inches off the ground. Who on earth came up with that idea?

One further infringement of our liberties under New Labour, and a serious threat to free speech. Every candidate has the right to have an electoral communication delivered free of charge. These have to be pre-vetted by the Post Office for, inter alia, libel. Since when has the Post Office, as opposed to a court of law, been qualified to decide what a candidate may or may not say? I feel rather insulted it found nothing wrong with my electoral communication. I am obviously not being radical enough.

The signs continue to look good. We held a meeting on Monday at the 120-capacity Daisyfields community centre. Three hundred people turned up, and we had to have speakers in a garden for the overflow. We had a webcast audience of more than 500, and two satellite channels were filming. I had so many lapel mic transmitters clipped to my belt that as I spoke my trousers kept falling down. I kept leaning with my hands in my pockets, hoping I looked casual as I struggled to get them back up. I got rapturous applause, so I might try to replicate the effect next time

*****

As you read this, the polls will be open. The voters of Blackburn will be streaming out in their happy thousands to vote for me and to consign Jack Straw to political oblivion. Or not, as the case may be.

The campaign continues to produce its lighter moments. A postman told one of my canvassers he was voting for that nice Mr Rigging. We were stumped by this, until we realised that our election communication is headed: "You can beat Labour vote rigging."

I was delighted to be approached by a whole crowd in the pub last night wanting my autograph. I was overwhelmed by my own popularity and thought I was home and dry. Then I discovered that they thought I was "that bloke that's shagging Sally on Corrie". I don't know who that actor is, but evidently he must be a man of great good looks and charisma. Now that Ian McKellen is on Coronation Street, I console myself that being mistaken for one of the cast is socially acceptable.

One of our slogans has been "British Bulldog, not Bush's Poodle", which has the advantage of confusing people entirely about the political direction we are coming from. This at least gets them to open the leaflet and read more. It was devised by Edward, who used to work for Saatchi and Saatchi. He claims it appeals to both left and right. It could, of course, alienate both instead. I suppose we'll soon know.

My mate Matt was canvassing when he was attacked by the two largest poodles imaginable. The unrepentant owner of these gruesome animals declared herself deeply offended by the jibe at poodles. Happily, the militant poodle front seems outnumbered by the gratified bulldog owners.

Getting a platform has proved difficult. The local council has failed to meet its legal obligation to provide public meeting rooms in schools, community centres, etc. We had Moazzam Begg on Sunday to talk about his detention in Guantanamo, and we had to hire a private ballroom. The council claimed they couldn't staff a public room over the bank holiday, but community centres were used by Straw for public meetings on the bank holiday Monday.

What's more, on the Saturday of the bank holiday weekend the Returning Officer tracked me down to Puccino's cafe, where he told me that there had been a complaint that my posters did not meet the legal requirement for a publishing imprint. I pointed out the publishing imprint to him, and he vanished. There seems to be no shortage of energy for stifling democracy, but less for promoting it.

Straw refuses to meet me on a platform. The cathedral organised a so-called hustings on Sunday from which I was barred. The BBC has rubbed salt into the wounds of its refusal to give me election coverage by putting in requests from four different programmes to interview me after the polls are closed. I did eventually get a confirmation that a central BBC decision had been taken not to cover my campaign. Helen Boaden, head of news and current affairs, replied that the BBC could not cover me because its regional political team "was unable to assess if I had significant electoral support". Why are they unable to assess it? What are they being paid for? So if anyone hopes to see me on election night, you will have to watch on ITV.

It seems to me essential that Straw is punished for the illegal war, for the decision that the intelligence services should regularly use information obtained under torture, for the dossier of lies on Iraqi WMD. At least in Blackburn Labour must pay. The argument that it did well on employment and health, as advanced by Polly Toynbee, is precisely the argument deployed in favour of Hitler and Mussolini. I don't see how any self-respecting person can vote Labour, no matter which orifice they cover with their fingers.

So how will we do? Well, surprisingly well. There is real anger at the war. People don't like liars. And Straw is plainly very worried. Unlike previous elections, he has not been out to marginals to support other candidates. Rather Gordon Brown, Robin Cook and even the Iraqi deputy prime minister have been here to bolster him. Neither the Lib Dems nor the Tories see this as winnable; they have not brought in a single big hitter. Of whom is he scared? Me.

Blackburn people have plenty to protest about. I have offered nothing but honesty and hard work. I have no idea if that might prove enough.

Anyone want a Green Goddess, slightly used?

Blackburn Campaign Interview with Paul Routledge

Craig Murray's Quixotic Blackburn campaign drew a great deal of media interest, including this 28 March 2005 interview with veteran left wing journalist Paul Routledge for the New Statesman.

Craig Murray, our troublesome former man in Tashkent, is at a loss to understand why he has not been charged under the Official Secrets Act. After all, he has disclosed secret diplomatic despatches from his time in the Uzbek capital, exposing torture and human rights abuses under the regime of President Islam Karimov - abuses that the Foreign Office ignored. And he's still spilling the beans: for good measure, the Khanabad military base, run by the US on the outskirts of Karshi, which is supposed to have only two air force squadrons and 1,200 ground troops, has "more of both, not acknowledged publicly. It's enormous, and it's intended to be permanent."

Now, sacked by the Foreign Office for speaking out against tyranny, Murray is investing some of his ?315,000 pay-off to stand as an independent candidate against the Foreign Secretary, Jack Straw, in his Lancashire seat of Blackburn.

The old cotton town is an unlikely setting for a conflict over foreign policy. It does not usually register events in the outside world. The Wars of the Roses passed it by. The English civil war made little impact, and even the class war failed to rouse much interest. Straw, moreover, won a majority of 9,200 in 2001, and the odds against bringing him down are daunting. However, his majority has been as low as 5,000; Straw's predecessor and mentor, Barbara Castle, once scraped in by 489 votes. And today, the Muslim vote, estimated at 20-25 per cent of the 73,000 electorate, is unlikely to support Labour en masse as before.

Murray believes he can be the grit in the oyster, taking up to 3,000 votes from Muslims and disgruntled Labour traditionalists. Arthur Scargill's Socialist Labour Party and the Socialist Alliance polled almost 1,100 at the last election - before the Iraq war, the mistreatment of Muslims at Guantanamo Bay and the threats from the Home Office minister Hazel Blears of increased stop-and-search of Asians.

"I think Straw is in trouble, I honestly do," says Murray. "And if he loses his seat because of foreign policy, that will make it impossible for Tony Blair to follow Bush if he decides to invade Syria or Iran . . . We can stop any war here in Blackburn."

Murray also wants to forestall a domestic strategy based on the "complete bollocks" of intelligence from the security services, particularly MI6. Until he encountered Foreign Office indifference that intelligence was being gleaned by means of torture in Uzbekistan, "I didn't realise fully that when they say this material is very useful, it doesn't mean that it is very true . . . They really didn't seem to care that it wasn't true, if it served their purpose."

Murray was born in Norfolk in 1958, the son of a gaming machine operator. After grammar school, he took a First in history at Dundee University and was president of the students' union. He was a Liberal then (and probably is now), and took the civil service exams only because he couldn't get a job in marketing. He was second secretary in Lagos in the late 1980s, first secretary in Warsaw after the Soviet downfall and deputy high commissioner to Ghana, before he was invited in 2002 to become the UK's ambassador to Uzbekistan. He said "yes", put down the phone, and took out the atlas to find where it was.

Foreign Office briefings gave him little idea of what to expect. "I felt like I had been asleep and woke up in the middle of The Quiet American. CIA people everywhere." Karimov, who became first secretary of the Uzbek Communist Party in 1989, has held the presidency of the former Soviet republic since 1991 - with the help of crooked elections and referendums. Murray denounced the regime as "not a functioning democracy" and exposed the barbaric tactics of the security apparat (which included boiling a man alive) just three months after he took up his post.

He was recalled, accused of granting UK visas in exchange for sex and of drunkenness - an easy allegation for a man who lists drinking as a recreation in Who's Who, and mentions his membership of the Dzien Dobry ("cheers") club in Poznan. Though the charges were dropped, Murray's return to Tashkent was short-lived, and he was brought back to London to face the consequences of his undiplomatic behaviour.

Britain was anxious not to embarrass the United States, which has poured men and materiel into Uzbekistan since 2002, turning a blind eye to Karimov's suppression of an ineffective Islamist revolt. The number of political prisoners is generally estimated at between 7,000 and 10,000, but Murray claims the true figure is twice that. Tashkent is the hub of central Asia, and the Americans want to hold on to the strategic advantage that the "war on terror" has given them in the region.

Murray, slightly portly and with a taste for three-piece suits, is becoming a figure on the intellectual protest scene. His character is the star of a new play for the Royal Court, Talking to Terrorists, which premieres outside London in April; in the autumn his book Should Not Be Known will be published. The title is from James Elroy Flecker's collection of poems The Golden Journey to Samarkand, which speaks of the "lust of knowing what should not be known". Murray also contemplates making a TV film debunking MI6.

Of Blackburn Rovers, enjoying their best FA Cup run in 40 years, Straw says: "I never make predictions. I just pray." Perhaps he should spend a bit more time on his knees in the next five weeks.

The Ambassador's Last Stand

In Blackburn the BBC followed Craig Murray to make a fly on the wall documentary "The Ambassador's Last Stand". Originally commissioned for Panorama, the screening date was changed three times and eventually it was put out late at night on BBC2.

The BBC producer of the documentary, John Sweeney, published this interview with Craig Murray on 19 September 2005.

It's early morning and Craig Murray -our former man in Uzbekistan -is making himself a cup of tea in a Blackburn semi during his doomed attempt to unseat the foreign secretary Jack Straw in May's general election. His towel slips and he is exposed, our nudest ambassador.

"Oops!" says Murray, "losing my dignity. Not to mention my towel. Careful where you're putting that camera. Children might be watching. Old ladies might faint with shock. Young ladies might faint with lust."

They might, but that seems unlikely. Murray is 46, and has the body of a devil sick of sin. But he does have a 25-year-old Uzbek girlfriend and a liking for a drink and talks openly about the joys of sex. So, you might say, no wonder Jack Straw's men fired him.

Being a sexual pervert, a crook or a drunk has never been an impediment to a fine career in the Foreign Office: Donald Maclean once defecated on the carpet during a party thrown by an American diplomat and it was all hushed up. Nothing untoward happened to the traitor until he upped sticks and defected to Moscow.

Today, one senior figure at King Charles Street is said to be a serial shagger - "everybody knows about it" -having allegedly bedded at least two female Labour MPs, and nobody has cut down his ration of Ferrero Rochers.

Although Murray admits he is a bit of a lad, he insists that he is not a drunk or a crook or a perv, and remains deeply wounded that the Foreign Office accused him of selling visas for sex, of being off his head on booze and stealing Her Majesty's dosh: "They hit me with 18 charges and I was cleared on all 18." His crime, he says, was to commit the sin of sins, to criticise the way America was running its war on terror, in private and in public.

He challenged the credibility of Uzbek intelligence given to the Americans and British, saying that it was based on torture. X and Y and Z were confessing to be major players in Al-Qaeda, said the raw material from the Uzbeks. Rubbish, said Murray, pointing out that in President Islam Karimov's neo-Stalinist central Asian despotism, they boil people alive, and worse.

In a series of telegrams to Straw, copied to MI6, the lawyers and all the senior players, Murray argued that a) intelligence based on torture was useless because a torture victim will confess to anything, and b) that it was morally wrong -"we are selling our souls for dross".

Straw saw the telegrams, says Murray, and came to the judgment that Her Majesty's government should continue relying on the boil-in-the-bag intelligence.

This issue wasn't academic for the ambassador. Within days of starting his job in Tashkent in 2002, photographs of a corpse landed on his desk. He sent them off to Britain, to be analysed by a Home Office pathologist.

The victim was a supporter of Hizb ut-Tahrir, a fundamentalist Islamic organisation but one that professes non-violence. Murray says: "The main finding was that this person had died from immersion in boiling liquid. And it was immersion, rather than splashing, because there was a clear tide-line around the upper torso and upper limbs and complete burns coverage underneath.

"Obviously the idea of someone being boiled to death is pretty horrific and that was one of the first eye-openers that I found in Uzbekistan."

Most British ambassadors would have huffed and puffed in private, and said nothing in public. Imagine the fuss, then, when Murray spoke his mind in a speech in Tashkent in October 2002. Lines such as "Uzbekistan is not a functioning democracy", "brutality is inherent" and just the mention of the secret police "boiling men to death" went down like a lead balloon. The uproar in central Asia was heard in Washington DC.

The Americans have a huge airbase there, just north of Afghanistan. What Murray said might have been true, but it was not "helpful" in the war on terror.

Murray is nothing if not smart. He had cleared his speech with the Foreign Office beforehand. Someone might have been very dim at King Charles Street, but they couldn't get Murray on procedure.

As the war in Iraq drew near, and Washington's rhetoric about Saddam's "torture and rape rooms" grew louder, Murray sent telegrams bemoaning "double standards".

"When it comes to the Karimov regime, systematic torture and rape appear to be treated as peccadilloes, not to affect the relationship and to be downplayed in the international (forums) ... I hope that once the present crisis is over we will make plain to the US, at senior level, our serious concern over their policy in Uzbekistan."

The irony here for Murray is that he says all he was doing was following new Labour's ethical foreign policy. The problem was, perhaps, that the policy had been dropped.

A stout patriot, in every sense of the phrase, Murray's contempt for what he calls the doublespeak that justified torture is based on a deep sense that Britishness should never have anything to do with electrodes on genitals. It is a remarkable passion for a diplomat and has caused him to lose his job, his lifestyle and, for a time, his sanity.

Murray said while stomping the streets of Blackburn: "I feel tremendously strongly about what this government has done in launching an illegal war, combined with the attacks on civil liberty at home, the portrayal of the Muslim community as being full of terrorists and the decision to obtain and use intelligence that was got under torture. This constitutes a real slide towards evil and people have a duty to try to stand up against it, and that's what I'm doing."

Murray's sacrifice was real. He loved his job. "I do often wish I was back in Uzbekistan, partly because I liked the people so much but mostly because I felt I was doing valuable work."

He also loved the lifestyle. "There was a very beautiful landscaped garden in Uzbekistan, a very wonderful swimming pool. It was very idyllic. I used to have people who hung up my clothes for me, and washed them and ironed them, and all that sort of stuff. Sadly, those days are gone."

And going bonkers wasn't fun. After the Foreign Office accused him of being a thieving, drunken sex maniac, he suffered a mental breakdown and was flown back to London and admitted to St Thomas's hospital. "I was determined to hold onto my self-respect. I wasn't going to admit to something that I hadn't done. But it's amazing how easy it is to break someone.

"I went into complete listlessness, apathy, I was crying, I couldn't see any way out. I couldn't tell anyone about it and I was actually brought back under medical supervision. For the first 10 days of that I was on suicide watch. That involved a large male nurse being with me, 24 hours a day, following me into the loo and that kind of thing. I tell you that if you're not suicidal before, you get suicidal pretty quickly when you are being followed into the loo by a large male nurse."

He got his marbles back, fought the Foreign Office, cleared his name and realised his career was over. He took early retirement and remains Jack Straw's least favourite critic. Thus far, the ever-nimble foreign secretary has avoided every single attempt by Murray to debate the issues one-to-one.

A bit like the Terminator, Murray staggers on, relentlessly, accusing Straw of complicity in torture -and that is a breach of article 4 of the United Nations convention against torture. Straw's line is that, "to the best of my knowledge", no intelligence he receives is based on torture, to which Murray says: "He is lying." The Foreign Office disagrees.

Murray's heroic failure when he stood in Blackburn against Straw is, like most tragedies, blackly comical. I will never forget the sight of Murray standing on top of the Green Goddess, the ancient army fire engine he bought for the campaign, and proclaiming in his rich baritone to elderly Lancashire ladies who looked the spitting image of Ena Sharples: "People have their fingernails ripped out, have electrodes attached to their genitals, are suffocated, drowned in the torture chambers ..."

He got fewer votes than the British National party. It was a miserable ending to a brave adventure as Straw's supporters booed Murray with special vehemence. "The guy from the BNP turned to me and said, 'They hate you more than me'."

The day we finished editing our film was 7/7. We were in a sound dub in central London, a few streets away from the Tavistock Square bus bomb. The sound engineer quipped: "It's a great film, John, but torturing Muslims is about to be Britain's number one Olympic sport."

It was a cruel joke, all the funnier because of the germ of

truth in it. If torturing some fanatic with a beard in Uzbekistan could prevent another 50 people being blown to smithereens on the Piccadilly line, why not? Murray replies: "No.

Torturing innocents is wrong. But torturing the guilty is wrong, too. If we in Britain change our mind about that, then at least we should have the honesty to say so. Torture is wrong, full stop."

At the forthcoming Labour party conference Straw will trot out his usual line: "The British government does not condone torture, full stop" - which is not quite the same thing, as he and Craig Murray know only too well.

Speech to Policy Exchange
28 June 2005

Opposition to New Labour led to courtship by more liberal elements of the Conservative Party. This speech was delivered to their leading think tank. The audience were somewhat nonplussed.

I'll concentrate this evening on the remit I was given - what the West has done wrong, in my view, what we should be doing to put it right. I'll start off with just a couple of facts. The first one comes from Human Rights Watch's report on the Andizhan massacre, which I'd recommend to you. They interviewed over fifty eye-witnesses; it's a very good report. And it wasn't just that the crowds were fired on, and fired on continually, and chased and fired on as they ran, on the May 13th, but afterwards Babur Square, where the main massacre happened, was sealed and the wounded were left lying, left overnight with no care, no attention, no medical treatment. And the next morning troops walked through the wounded finishing them off with shots to the head.

To anyone who knows Uzbekistan it is conceivable, though extremely unlikely, that troops could have opened fire on the 13th due to some situation that developed and got out of control locally. But it is completely inconceivable that twenty-four hours later troops would be walking through the streets shooting people without having authority right from the top of what is an extremely efficient totalitarian dictatorship.

I'll give you another interesting fact. One of the Uzbek opposition leaders, a gentleman who's in exile, Muhammed Salih, fought the only vaguely democratic election that President Karimov has ever faced when he opposed him in the presidential election in, I think, '92. It wasn't a very democratic election. The media was

100% government controlled. Salih had no access and no coverage except complete vilifications. His supporters were subject to violence and arrest and the polls were rigged in every conceivable way. He still officially got about 15% of the vote, which was quite extraordinary in the circumstances. He now lives in exile in Germany.

Last August when I was still British Ambassador I suggested that we invite him to the Foreign Office to perhaps meet a junior minister or senior officials. My suggestion was greeted with stunned horror in the Foreign Office, where I was told - Did I not know that he'd been convicted of terrorism? I said, 'nobody, but nobody, believes Muhammed Salih is a terrorist. It's a propaganda conviction.' The Foreign Office checked with its research analysts, who confirmed that absolutely nobody thinks Muhammed Salih is a terrorist. I was then told that OK, he may not be a terrorist but he has been convicted of terrorism and therefore it would be awful insulting to President Karimov, were we to speak to him. And I was also told off for having even suggested it, and Muhammed Salih was not invited to meet anyone in the Foreign Office.

Subsequently last autumn, PEN, the campaign group for imprisoned writers, and the BBC World Service, invited Muhammed Salih to the UK anyway, and the government refused him a visa. They did so on the grounds that he might seek to illegally immigrate here. The facts are that he already has political asylum in Germany, he lives in Germany with his family, he speaks German and he doesn't speak English - but it was plainly just not on to have anyone from the democratic Uzbek opposition walking around the streets of London, because it might upset our dear friend Mr Karimov. And to my knowledge still to this day, certainly since September 11th 2001, neither ministers nor senior officials in the Foreign Office have met anyone from the

Uzbek opposition.

This is not typical of the way the Foreign Office works. The Foreign Office is usually very open to meeting democratic opposition figures from dictatorial states. And I give it to you as an example of the way the Foreign Office's attitude, the British Government's attitude to Uzbekistan does not stand up anywhere near official British Government policy on democracy and human rights.

The situation in Uzbekistan is dire. There is, I think, general agreement among academic authorities, that poverty is increasing, that the major drive behind events in Andizhan, the major cause of the unrest, the reason taxi drivers are so grumbly, is that people have declining access to household goods and declining diet and yet the West fails to stand up to the reality of the situation. The IMF and the World Bank still now, today, will tell you that the economic growth rate in Uzbekistan this year is 4.4%. The IMF and the World Bank have given a positive growth rate for Uzbekistan every year since 1993 - for most of which time, and certainly for the last ten of those years, the economy has been in headlong decline. Interestingly, if you look another lot of World Bank figures they tell you that in 2003 total Uzbek GDP was $9.9 billion whereas in 1993 it was it was $13.1 billion. Which means that it had declined by 30% in the ten year period during which it had increased every year.

This is absolutely typical of the failure of the West to tackle or even acknowledge what is happening in Uzbekistan. When the Uzbek government say to the IMF delegation 'our automotive production is up by 12%, our oil and gas production is up by 25%, our agricultural production is up by 17%', the IMF don't say 'you're lying,' which would be the honest response. They say 'oh yes, hmm.' And they hum and hah and they negotiate a bit, which is much more than the UN do.

The UN this year will give you just the official Uzbek government figure, which is of economic growth of 8.9%. You'll find that on the UNDP website. The IMF, to be fair to them, don't agree with that. They just accept a figure, after a little bit of negotiation, that somewhere in between the truth and the Uzbek government figure - but a lot closer to the Uzbek government figure than the truth. So we have this paradise, where people are enjoying much better rates of economic growth then any of the developed world, but where at the same time everyone is getting poorer and the West doesn't face the fact.

The same is true of our approach to the internal situation. 'Muhammed Salih is a terrorist, so we don't meet him.' 'He's not a terrorist.' 'Well, OK, maybe.' In March of 2004 there were - and you'll find this reported in pretty well every authority including academic authorities - there were a series of suicide bombings in Tashkent. Each one, according to the Procurator General of Uzbekistan - speaking at a press conference to which the diplomatic corps and the media were invited - each one was committed using a suicide belt containing an equivalent of 2 kilos of TNT; and in each about thirty or forty people were killed.

There are some difficulties with this. I got myself to the site of each of the blasts within hours, and in one case within forty minutes, of the blast going off. One of them took place in an enclosed courtyard not that much bigger than this room. It had a tree in the middle, buildings round, and not a pane of glass was shattered, and not a twig was torn from the tree. Apparently six policemen had just died there in a bomb blast.

At one of the other places there was supposed to have been a car bomb. I was there within two hours. No sign of any blast whatsoever.

The facts did not in the least bit relate to the stories. I

reported this back to London, who didn't want to know this. It was much more convenient that it was Al Qaeda and this came, very conveniently actually, one week before Colin Powell had to make his determination on whether Uzbekistan met the Human Rights criteria for continued UN aid.

But much more interestingly we had intelligence material. We had telephone intercepts. Satellite telephone calls from known senior Al Qaeda officers in the Middle East and in Pakistan - and incidentally if anyone thinks I'm revealing a secret and they don't know their phones are tapped, they must be extremely naive people. And they were saying to each other 'what the hell is happening in Tashkent? Bombs are going off in Tashkent. Does anyone know what's happening?' This was Al Qaeda talking to each other. These were actually NSA American security intercepts.

Despite that, the next day Colin Powell stands up and says 'Al Qaeda have launched a dastardly attack on our great ally, President Karimov. We must give more support to Uzbekistan.' And he knew he was lying. That's what I'm telling you. We knew that intelligence wasn't true, because we knew Al Qaeda didn't know what was happening in Tashkent.

The truth is that the West has got itself into bed with an absolutely appalling dictatorship, and a dictatorship which is not going to reform.

I'd only been in Tashkent for a very few weeks when I attended the opening of Freedom House in Uzbekistan. The American Ambassador got up and welcomed the abolition of censorship and welcomed the increase in private ownership of enterprises and welcomed something else, and none of those things had happened at all. They were all entirely fictitious. They were simply untrue; they were lies. I got up and I said Uzbekistan is not a functioning democracy, neither is it moving in the direction of a democracy; a fact which was actually self-evidently true but contradicted everything the American Ambassador had just said. And this capacity for delusion on the part of the West has to be tackled.

You'll see for example claims from Uzbekistan that now 35% of GDP is in the private sector. Completely untrue. Claims about the privatisation of farming. They're based on the sub-division of state farms into smaller state farm units, which are simply accounting transactions which actually aren't setting up any kind of market and have no effect whatsoever. The truth is that Uzbekistan is still a country where sixty percent of the population live on state farms, on kolkhoz, where they can't leave the farm. It's a country which maintains not just exit visas but internal movement visas. It's a country where you can't go five miles on any road in the country without encountering a police road check. If you're born on the farm you'll die on the farm in most cases. It's a country where an enslaved population suffers at the hand of an entirely rapacious government that has no intention of reforming: no intention of reforming.

And so far, because we decided post September 11th that Karimov was our great ally in the region against Islamic fundamentalism, we've maintained our support on the basis of deluding ourselves that he is reforming, that he is changing. If you're going to continue to maintain, as this government does, that its policy is one of constructive engagement - which it calls now 'critical engagement' in order to avoid comparison with Mrs. Thatcher's policy towards South Africa - you have to show progress for your critical engagement, and there isn't any.

There is no free media in Uzbekistan: None. There is no legal opposition in Uzbekistan: None. On 26th December parliamentary elections were held in Uzbekistan in which the opposition parties were not allowed to compete. There is no religious freedom in Uzbekistan. And the last couple of weeks, it's worth noting, have seen a renewed clampdown on Protestant churches, with a number of new arrests of Protestant ministers, so it's not only Islamists who suffer. It's really a disaster.

How do we make it better? Well I would say first of all we face the facts. We face the facts. We face the facts as I've outlined them to you. We stop hiding behind this delusion that reform is happening, Karimov is a secret reformist who's just hidden it very well for the last fifteen years. We stop accepting the propaganda about all opposition being Islamists.

I agree absolutely about the huge potential for violence because there is no opposition, but that's because we have done nothing to help the opposition. We've put all our eggs in the Karimov basket. Just as I couldn't get Salih a visa to come and talk to our ministers, I couldn't get any money at all to help Democratic Forum, an opposition grouping which tried to get going last year, bringing together the various democratic opposition elements in Uzbekistan. Neither the Foreign Office nor the US government was in the least bit interested. The sad thing is that this is actually going to lead to Islamic extremism in a country which has had very little of it in the past, because people have no alternative. They're not given any kind of Western alternative. And it's a policy which, in itself, will build a hatred of the West, because we are seen as backing and supporting a dictator who is himself hated by his own people. It's a self-defeating policy on our side.

Let me put it to you bluntly. If someone took my brother and boiled him to death, I know what I'd do. We are creating terrorism ourselves by our foolish refusal to face up to what kind of man Karimov is, and the fact that this is not a government with which you can do business in the normal way. There are creative ways of helping democratic opposition to flourish. For example, in Bishkek [the capital of Kyrgyzstan], the Americans put in a printing press, in order to help encourage free media. No initiatives of that kind have been undertaken in Uzbekistan.

And we also have to look at what it does to international institutions, to allow in them members who simply do not agree with the basic tenets of the organisation. Uzbekistan is a member of the OSCE for example. Uzbekistan believes in none of the fundamental tents of the OSCE. It doesn't believe in democracy, has no intention of ever becoming a democracy. It doesn't believe in economic reform. Why is it in? It's not in Europe anyway. Why is it in? It's in because it's part of the former Soviet Union. But how can the OSCE continue to have a member which actually doesn't hold to the rules of the club or intend to hold to the rules of the club? It's not a question of how fast it's moving in the right direction; it's the fact that if it's moving in any direction, it's the wrong direction.

The only institution that has actually faced this squarely is the EBRD - which was forced to do so because it held its AGM in Tashkent in 2003 and completely uniquely, I believe, in its history, decided to limit lending to Uzbekistan on the basis of its poor record on human rights and democracy, in line with article 1 of its charter. For once, the EBRD actually decided to follow its own charter and insist that members stick to the rules or effectively be suspended. And in effect Uzbekistan was suspended.

NATO similarly. Uzbekistan is in the Partnership for Peace. It absolutely sickens me that British troops were last year - and I don't just mean training for officers, though we do that in the UK for Uzbek officers - British troops were last year training alongside Uzbek troops in Uzbekistan in company strength, in formation, doing

NATO P4P peacekeeping exercises. British troops were quite possibly training alongside some of the soldiers who shot wounded people in the head as they lay oh the ground in Andizhan

What signals have we sent to Karimov since? Well, though Karimov has been killing people for years - he's had lots of practice - he hasn't generally killed 700 people at once. Today he'll be thinking that even if you kill 700 opponents at once, nothing bad happens to you, because nothing has. Why do we treat Lukashenko and Mugabe as pariahs, subject to personal travel restrictions, to a range of targeted sanctions, but not Karimov? The answer to this, of course, is an obsession with the Karshi-Khanabad airbase, as one of the most important of Rumsfeld's 'lily-pads' - bases which can be rapidly expanded, and from which massive military force can be quickly projected into any area of what they call the Wider Middle East in the Pentagon - which means the Middle East, the Caucasus and Central Asia, which is of course the great band of oil and gas reserves.

But is it worth the candle? Are we really getting such a benefit? I can tell you for certain that part of American thinking was that if you are looking at contingencies regarding Iran, it would cause enormous difficulty to use bases out of Afghanistan to attack Iran, enormous difficulty in terms of Afghan public opinion, but public opinion had never been a factor that needed to be considered in Uzbekistan.

But this is war on terrorism thinking, this idea that Karimov is on our side, that he's an ally, that Uzbekistan is an ally, that Uzbekistan is part of the coalition of the willing. I was under instruction to refer to Uzbekistan as an ally every time I spoke in public, whatever I was saying. It didn't matter what subject, I had to start off 'We enormously appreciate Uzbekistan's contribution to the coalition in Iraq; Uzbekistan our great ally in the

War on Terror. Now I'm here to open this nursery school' or whatever. That 'you're with us or against us' thinking, the idea that it doesn't matter how nasty you are, that the world is divided into two camps, there's us, the civilised people of the universe, and there's all those nasty rather damned Muslim people; that thinking, which dominates American policy, is what has driven Western policy towards Uzbekistan, and unless we get out of it we're going to bring disaster both on the people of Uzbekistan and upon ourselves.
Thank you.

The 7/7 London Bombings and Their Causes

Blog article 19 July 2005. This was the first time Craig Murray had used his blog as a primary means of communication rather than to repost other material. At this time he only had about 1,200 readers daily.

There is a heated discussion in progress at the moment about whether the war in Iraq caused the London bombings. Jack Straw was quoted yesterday dismissing the notion that it had anything to do with Iraq, pointing out that bombers had also struck in countries which did not have troops in Iraq. Tony Blair has made the point that on September 11 2001 Iraq had not yet been attacked. Which is true, although he and Bush had already agreed to do so.

But unlike the bombs in New York and Turkey, these involved young British Muslims. To pretend that the anger of young British Muslims is not stoked by Blair's foreign policy is just absolute nonsense. Following along with the George Bush international agenda, including the attack on Iraq, has made us deeply unpopular with Muslims everywhere.

On 18 March 2003 I sent Jack Straw an official telegram from Tashkent about US foreign policy in Central Asia, and our support for it. An extract reads:

4. Democracy and human rights are, despite their protestations to the contrary, in practice a long way down the US agenda here. Aid this year will be slightly less, but there is no intention to introduce any meaningful conditionality. Nobody can believe this level of aid - more than US aid to all of West Africa - is related to comparative developmental need as opposed to political support for Karimov. While the US makes token and low-level references to human rights to appease domestic opinion, they view Karimov's vicious regime as a bastion against fundamentalism. He - and they - are in fact creating fundamentalism. When the US gives this much support to a regime that tortures people to death for having a beard or praying five times a day, is it any surprise that Muslims come to hate the West?

It is Iraq, but not just Iraq. It is a foreign policy of oil grab cloaked in hypocrisy, and the impact of that policy on Muslims, that has caused this hate. And that is squarely the fault of Blair and Straw.

None of which justifies the terror. It is probable that most of the people who got killed and injured on 7 July were opposed to Blair and Bush. Only 23% of eligible British adults voted for New Labour. Several of the victims will have marched against the war. Violence just begets more violence.

Nor will it help to rush through yet more legislation restricting civil liberties. It is already against the law to incite someone to commit terrorism. An offence of 'indirect incitement', now proposed, sounds very dangerous indeed. It could be just what is needed to silence critics like us.

But perhaps most risible is the government's claim that the new legislation is needed to 'prevent further terrorism'. That you do that by legislation is laughable.

It is also hard to equate with the other government line, that attacks on London are 'inevitable'. They are not. Had we not thrown our lot in with Bush, we would not have been attacked. Terrorism is a politically motivated act by human beings. It is not a natural phenomenon like the wind.

We should certainly not change our foreign policy in response to terrorism. We should change it because it was seriously misguided in the first place, and is bringing on us consequences that many of us saw and predicted.

Perpetual War

In the aftermath of the 7/7 bombings, Brazilian electrician Jean Charles De Menezes was shot to death – seven times in the head – by armed police officers who suspected him of being a terrorist purely because he emerged from the same apartment block as a suspect (who also turned out not to be a terrorist either). This operation was masterminded by Cressida Dick, later to be appointed by Theresa May as Head of the Metropolitan Police. Blog article 28 July 2005.

Subsequent evidence found that the situation was even worse than portrayed here. Reports that Menezes had sought to run away were police disinformation. He had been shot dead while innocently seated on the tube train.

What is most worrying about the sad death of the Brazilian Mr Jean Charles de Menezes, shot to death by police on the tube, is that it is used by the government to further ratchet up the climate of fear. While regretting the death, Jack Straw tells us that the "Shoot to kill" policy must remain, while Sir Ian Blair says that more innocent deaths cannot be ruled out. All this boosts the politics of fear, talking up the perpetual war scenario that justifies increased government authoritarianism.

Our tactics for dealing with potential suicide bombers are apparently borrowed from the Israelis. This is appalling. It is not so long ago that the UK was horrified by pictures of a fourteen year old girl being shot down at an Israeli checkpoint, and an Israeli officer emptying a magazine into her head. Now we are adopting precisely the same tactics ourselves ' the unarmed Mr Menezes took eight bullets to the head, not the five originally reported.

What is more, we are now adopting Israeli rhetoric. Any attempt to explain or understand the phenomenon of terrorism is dismissed as "justifying" or "excusing" it. Blair rants that Muslim anger has nothing to do with Iraq, or Guantanamo Bay, or Abu Ghraib, or our support for torturers of Muslims like Karimov. It is rather a spontaneous development, sufficient unto itself, arising in a vacuum from the evil teachings of Wahhabism.

But the truth is that Muslim hatred feeds on some very real injustices. That in no way justifies or excuses acts of terror, which are warped and evil. But the growth of that evil is not, as Blair and Bush appear to believe, the spontaneous work of the devil. There are a few masterminds of terror who are simply psychopaths. But by removing injustice we can remove their ability to recruit, and to operate within a sympathetic community milieu. Announcing a firm intention to withdraw troops soon from Iraq would be a start. Announcing an end to all government to government co-operation with the Uzbek regime would be another good move. We need to reduce the causes of tension.

What will not help is the Blair proposal to introduce detention without charge for three months for terrorist suspects. Over 1200 people have been arrested under government anti-terrorism legislation. Only 18 have actually been convicted ' and only a handful of them on anything to do with terrorism. Most were found to have some minor criminal involvement.

Almost all of these were Muslims. Nearly all were innocent and released after the current fourteen days. Holding large quantities of innocent Muslims now for three months is hardly going to reduce tension. Let us not forget that one of the first reactions to the 7 July bombings was to arrange the arrest by Egyptian authorities of a Leeds chemist on holiday there. This was trumpeted on the front pages by our press as a great example of international intelligence co-operation against terror. There has been much less ' indeed almost no ' coverage of the fact he was found to have no connection at all to the bombs. He just happened to be a Muslim, from Leeds, a pharmacist (Aha! Potential Bomb Maker!) and to have gone on holiday at the time of the bombings. His was one of hundreds of British Muslim names falsely publicised in the UK media in the last three years as part of Al-Qaida.

Do not forget that on the afternoon of poor Mr Menezes' death, the Evening Standard carried the massive triumphalist headline "LONDON BOMBER SHOT DEAD". The Standard has not apologised.

There is another point that has not been made about Mr Menezes' death. He died because of his skin colour. As a Brazilian, his skin tone was not so different from that of the average British Muslim. Had someone with a complexion as white as mine been running around on the underground, they would not have been gunned down by the police.

Of course, Mr Menezes almost certainly died in terror having absolutely no idea who was chasing him. He was not asked to stop by uniformed police. He was suddenly chased by men in plainclothes waving guns. Is it surprising he ran? An eyewitness said that the police did not pull on Baseball caps saying "Police" until after he started running from them. At which point, chased by men with guns, he probably did not spend much time looking back and admiring his pursuers' headgear. He jumped on a tube, tripped and they shot him dead.

It is time we pulled back from this. To declare this part of an unending war, and the new normality we should live with, shows what a failed and irresponsible government we now have.

The Killing of Jean Charles De Menezes

Once police lies about the killing became clear, this article followed on 17 August 2005. Craig Murray was now becoming viewed as well outside the political mainstream.

I am not sure which scares me most - the way the police murdered Jean Charles de Menezes, or the lies they told about it afterwards. It is worth bearing in mind that when the Police and the Home Office went into overdrive to spin their dramatic falsehoods - that he vaulted the ticket barrier, ran through the station, wore a padded jacket and leapt onto the train - they still thought they had killed a terrorist, not a Brazilian electrician.

We now know that Mr Menezes had a ticket and passed the barrier the normal way, walked quietly through the station, picked up a newspaper, boarded the train quietly and sat down. He was then pinioned by a policeman and shot at eleven times by at least two others while immobilised in his seat.

That makes it not just an unlawful killing, but plain murder. And it would still be murder even if Mr Menezes was indeed a terrorist. That was unequivocally established by the Death on the Rock case, where the European Court ruled that it was illegal to assassinate IRA terrorists in cold blood in Gibraltar, whether or not they were engaged in a bombing operation.

The government are acutely aware of that precedent. That is why the lies about his bizarre behaviour were so quickly concocted, and assiduously spread. They did so with the help of a compliant media establishment that repeated these lies ad nauseam to an excited public. And of course, the liar in chief was Sir Ian Blair himself. He must now resign immediately. I have never believed in eugenics, but the evidence of the unique propensity to lying of the clan Blair is pretty compelling, though I confess my sample of two is statistically insignificant.

One of my chief allies in fighting for human rights in Uzbekistan was Professor Douwe Korff, a key member of the legal team that brought the British government to book over Death on the Rock. It is typical of this government that Charles Clark's reaction in his Evening Standard interview is to threaten British judges with new legislation to restrict their power to defend liberty. He also specifically threatened legislation to remove us from European Court jurisdiction ' no more Death on the Rock cases, then.

You could read about Douwe and I working in Uzbekistan in my forthcoming book, except that I have now received four letters and last evening a phone call from the Foreign and Commonwealth Office to tell me I can't publish it. It tells of Jack Straw's decision that MI6 should use intelligence obtained under torture by foreign intelligence agencies. They don't want you to know that. I had hoped that Straw's decision was an isolated bit of over-zealousness.

I now know that it was part of a systematic lowering of our standards on human rights across the board. Blair is, beyond denial, leading the most authoritarian government since Lord Liverpool In fact Blair's proposals outdo for sheer illiberalism the notorious Six Acts, which every schoolboy for generations learnt of as the most heinous assault on British liberties, happily overcome.

Blair's media support is of two sorts. The right wing press share this analysis, but applaud it. They have the most populist right wing leader in British history, and are delighted. On the other side The Blair project cheerleaders who dominate the Guardian are stuck with their monstrous delusions.

The BBC remains cowed by the Gilligan affair, and large job losses. The fact that Gilligan told the truth - there were no Iraqi WMD - perversely diminished rather than increased their confidence. Telling the truth gets you shafted. Toeing Tony's line gets you promoted.

Tony Blair's new raft of 'Anti-terrorist' proposals includes deporting people for visiting certain bookshops and websites. Police continued their policy of ramping up media hype by smashing open, for the cameras, the door of a Muslim bookshop in Leeds. The owners had actually given them the keys and invited them to look around. No propaganda value in that, so out came the battering ram.

The media have carried rubbish in screaming headlines about the bomb attacks on 7 and 21 July. They were perpetrated by Al Qaida, they were funded from Pakistan, the two groups were linked. All rubbish. And of course we had Tony Blair's repeated assertion that anger at our invasion of Iraq was in no way the cause. To understand was to excuse.

I condemn terrorism unequivocally. It is in every sense immoral and unreasoned. But it is not a natural phenomenon like the Birmingham tornado - Blair's actions provoked it. The invasion of Iraq based on a tissue of lies, the co-operation with security services of regimes that practice torture throughout the Muslim World, the support for Bush and Sharon on settlements policy, the imprisonments without trial and other attacks on liberty in the UK.

After the 9/11 attacks, I recall the general reaction of the British intelligentsia was to ask why the Americans failed to understand what it was that caused them to be hated in much of the rest of the World. In our own hurt following the London bombings, we are making the same mistake.

It will be little comfort to the family and friends of Mr Menezes, but there is some hope that his death and the exposure of the spin that surrounded it will cause some reaction to the way this country is headed.

It is essential to the survival of liberty in this country that the killers of Mr Menezes stand in the dock. Doubtless the press will mount a campaign to defend them. Isn't it time we were given their names? I don't recall the identities of other alleged killers such as Barry Bolsara or Peter Sutcliffe being protected before their trial. The police have happily given out the name of several people who turned out to be completely uninvolved, including a Leeds Muslim chemist who went on holiday to Egypt (dead suspicious).

Let's have the names of the killers. At least we can avoid sitting next to them on the tube. Given the manner of cold-blooded execution, I suspect they may turn out to be SAS or MI5. But the blame must not stop with the men who pulled the triggers. Nor does it lie solely with the people that provided the so-called intelligence identifying Mr Menezes. The real blame lies with those who sanctioned the 'shoot to kill' policy defended in such macho fashion by Jack Straw and Charles Clarke.

They must now resign. British liberty will not recover until Charles Clarke and Ian Blair stand in the dock for their part in this murder.

Robin Cook

Reaction to the unexpected death of Robin Cook while hill-walking, 8 August 2005.

I turned on my television to watch the news, and when it warmed into life, was surprised to see myself looking at a picture of Raigmore Hospital in Inverness.

For many years my parents lived close to Raigmore, at Incheswood, and that was the road from which the BBC were taking their picture. I have many happy memories of Inverness, and the hospital itself is a wonderful facility with cheerful and helpful staff. But I visited both my father and my grandfather in that hospital shortly before their deaths, and a chill enters my heart when I see it.

I now learnt of the death of Robin Cook, and felt a real sorrow.

I was one of a few enthusiasts in the Foreign and Commonwealth Office who welcomed the arrival of Robin Cook as Foreign Secretary and his declaration of an 'Ethical foreign policy'. The majority were hostile and cynical, but not nearly so much as was Tony Blair.

Within a very few weeks, Blair arranged Robin Cook's defeat at Cabinet when Cook wanted to stop the export of British Aerospace Hawk jets to the Suharto regime of Indonesia, which has a strong history of vicious repression of its disparate peoples. I was told by a Cabinet Minister who sided with Cook, that Blair managed Cook's cabinet defeat in as confrontational and humiliating a manner as possible.

Plainly there would be no ethical foreign policy under Blair, and 'New Labour' would be even snugger in bed with the arms industry than the old version. One of Blair's lead men on Hawks to Indonesia was Jack Straw, who declared in the register of members' interests that

50% of his election expenses had been paid by Lord Taylor, a Director of British Aerospace.

By one of life's sad ironies I was closely involved in an episode which held the ethical foreign policy up to media ridicule, from which it never recovered. A mercenary outfit called Sandline claimed to have been given the go-ahead by the FCO to ship weapons to Sierra Leone, to help President Kabbah recover his country from rebels. The problem was this breached a UN arms embargo. Both the Tory media and the pro-Blair Murdoch media had a frenzy, attacking Cook for claiming to be ethical while breaching UN law.

In fact, while Sandline had close connections with the British High Commission in Sierra Leone, they were simply lying about being given permission to ship arms. I can say that with certainty, because it was I they claimed gave the permission.

The storm passed, but ethical foreign policy disappeared as a term of art. The crisis brought me into closer and more intense personal contact with Robin Cook than I might normally have expected, and for that I am grateful.

His famous gnomic and ginger appearance is much commented upon, but I have never seen anyone describe his eyes, which is a pity. He had really startling eyes, of an extraordinarily light, bright, limpid blue. They absolutely held you, and as you spoke they were searching you out. I found him both funny and kind.

He had his faults. Very self-obsessed, the first time I ever met him I was kept waiting in his outer office for over three hours. No respecter of persons, he famously once did much the same to Princess Diana (well, maybe not three hours, but a lot longer than she was used to).

I met him again in Ghana, when he accompanied the Queen on a State Visit. He got so deeply into a conversation with a journalist that he missed the convoy as it departed from a Durbar, and had to be rescued from the massive crowds, having apparently lost interest in what the Queen and the Government of Ghana might be doing.

At that time, he was interviewing for a new Private Secretary. Deciding that this would be a useful way to fill out the hours spent as a courtier, he had the candidates flown out to Ghana at public expense to be interviewed ' including at least one candidate, then Head of the FCO's United Nations Department, whose London office was a thirty second walk from his.

So I observed him as self-centred and irascible, but at the same time kind, witty and deeply intelligent. I agreed with him on ethical foreign policy, and on the Iraq war. But where we will now miss his influence most of all, was his passionate commitment to individual liberty and balanced democracy.

Cook was the country's most influential advocate of proportional representation, the surest safeguard against abuse of power by narrow and unrepresentative government. He also wanted to see executive authority checked by a powerful and fully elected House of Lords. This was the great work of his second ministerial post, as Leader of the House. It should not be forgotten that just as Blair deliberately blocked Cook over ethical foreign policy, so he blocked an elected House of Lords. And Blair blocked it for exactly the reason Cook wanted it, because it would be a brake on the Prime Minister's authority.

It amazes me that, when Blair made clear he wanted a largely appointed House of Lords, most people still didn't tumble to just how power-mad the man is. Now we face proposals to hold people for three months without charge, and to deport people for entering the wrong bookshop or visiting the wrong website. We are to accept 'assurances' from murderous regimes that they won't torture or kill dissidents we hand over to them.

Blair bangs on as if it wasn't already illegal to be a terrorist, to kill people, to make or supply bombs or assist those who do. It is noteworthy that the alleged London bomber now charged is facing longstanding laws, like murder and conspiracy to murder, without any need for the raft of new legislation already in place, let alone Blair's latest proposals.

What kind of society are we turning into? Blair talks of designating suspect bookshops, and I have just received my fourth official letter from the government reminding me that my own book, which I haven't even finished yet, is banned from being published.

Robin Cook was a man of principle and lover of liberty, and he hated all of this. The last, brilliant, Guardian article I read by him was arguing against purchasing a replacement for trident missiles, while claiming that Blair had already taken that decision. He also stated baldly that the policy of Bush and Blair was creating terrorism, not defeating it.

These are the most dangerous times for liberty in the UK since the government of Lord Liverpool. Those of us who believe freedom is important, face a huge battle over many years, and against great odds. We have lost our best leader.

Fighting for Civil Liberties

By September 2005 The British Government was becoming more open in its use of intelligence from torture, and was also pushing a whole raft of measures designed to restrict civil liberties. Craig Murray was convinced that this was a struggle to maintain the fundamental tenets of liberal democracy against an increasing tide of corporate friendly authoritarianism.

This article of 21 October 2005 marks his increased focus on this issue. A slightly amended version appeared in the Independent on 27 October.

Before the House of Lords this week the government has been arguing for the right to act on intelligence obtained by torture abroad. Channel 4 has obtained the statement to the Law Lords by the head of MI5, Eliza Manningham-Butler. In effect she argues that torture works. It foiled the famous ricin plot.

She omits to mention that no more ricin was found than is the naturally occurring base level in your house or mine - or indeed that no poison of any kind was found. Nor does she recall that there has never been a successful large scale poisoning with ricin. But let us leave that for now.

She argues, in effect, that we need to get intelligence from foreign security services, to fight terrorism. And if they torture, so what? Her chief falsehood is our pretence that we don't know what happens in their dungeons. We do. And it is a dreadful story. Manningham-Butler is so fastidious she even avoids using the word 'Torture' at all in her evidence. Let alone the reality to which she turns such a carefully blind eye.

Uzbekistan is one of those security services from whose 'friendly liaison' services we obtained information. And

I will tell you what torture means. It means the woman who was raped with a broken bottle in both vagina and anus, and who died after ten days of agony. It means the old man suspended by wrist shackles from the ceiling while his children were beaten to a pulp before his eyes. It means the man whose fingernails were pulled before his face was beaten and he was immersed to his armpits in boiling liquid. It means the eighteen year old whose knees and elbows were smashed, his hand immersed in boiling liquid until the skin came away and the flesh started to peel from the bone, before the back of his skull was stove in.

These are all real cases from the Uzbek security services which we viewed as friendly liaison, and from which we obtained regular intelligence, in the Uzbek case via the CIA. A month ago that liaison relationship was stopped - not by us, but by the Uzbeks. But as Manningham-Buller sets out, we continue to maintain our position as customer to torturers in Saudi Arabia, Egypt, Algeria, Jordan, Morocco and many other places.

The key point is that none of the above Uzbek victims were terrorists at all. The great majority of those who suffer torture at the hands of these regimes are not terrorists, but political opponents. And the scale of this torture is vast. In Uzbekistan alone thousands, not hundreds, of innocent men, women and children suffer torture every year. Across Manningham-Buller's web of friendly intelligence agencies, the number may reach tens of thousands. Can our security really be based on such widespread inhumanity, or is that not part of the grievance that feeds terrorism? Every year the Uzbek government kills many times more innocent people than would realistically have died, even if someone had been able to scrape ricin out of their saucepan. Do those deaths not matter?

How many foreign Muslim lives is one British life worth?

These other governments know that our security services lap up information from their torture chambers. This practical condoning more than cancels out any weasel words on human rights which the Foreign Office may issue.

In fact, the case for the efficacy of torture intelligence is not nearly as clear-cut as Manningham-Buller makes out. Much dross comes out of the torture chambers. History should tell us that under torture people would choke out an admission that they had joined their neighbours in flying on broomsticks with cats. The narrative we get is the precise narrative that the foreign intelligence agency wishes us to hear. They often have their own agenda to plug.

A final thought. Manningham-Buller is arguing from the efficiency of torture in preventing a terrorist plot. If that argument is accepted, then in logic there is no reason to rely on foreign intermediaries. Why don't we do our own torturing at home? James VI and I abolished torture ' New Labour are making the first attempt in English courts to justify Government use of torture information. Why stop there? Why can't the agencies work over terrorist suspects?

I seem to recall that we tried that approach with the Birmingham 6 and the Guildford 4, and look where that got us.

The Security Services want us to be able to use information from torture. That should come as no surprise. From Sir Thomas Walsingham on, the profession attracts people not squeamish about the smell of seared flesh from the branding iron. That is why we have a judiciary to protect us. I pray that they do.

The Official Secrets Act

Following government attempts to censor and then prohibit the release of his memoir Murder in Samarkand, Craig Murray released thirteen of the classified documents onto the internet, together with an appeal for help to which 4,000 bloggers and other websites responded by publishing them, making it impossible to suppress.

Having faced down written threats from Treasury Solicitors to prosecute him under the Official Secrets Act, on 3 January 2006 Murray declared that he had made this famous and draconian legislation a dead letter.

It has come as a surprise to some that I am not currently a guest of Her Majesty. It is plainly a disappointment to others, particularly the trolls who have been gleefully predicting on Lenin's Tomb [blog] that the agents of the state will come and get us.

We have published what were, undoubtedly, classified British government documents. Under the notorious Official Secrets Act that is an offence, and everyone connected with it is plainly guilty. There is no public interest defence.

But there are problems with the Official Secrets Act. Despite New Labour attempts to roll them back, British criminal trials still involve juries, and they are reluctant to convict in OSA trials, where they often sympathise with the motives of the defendant. Clive Ponting was acquitted after leaking that the Belgrano was heading home when we sank it. The jury acquitted him, against the clear direction of the judge. And that was in the context of the Falklands War, which the British public supported. What chance of a conviction in the context of the Iraq war, which the British public oppose?

Katharine Gunn released details of GCHQ's involvement with the NSA in bugging UN delegations in New York, and the government withdrew the charges against her rather than face a trial.

There is still time, but to date we haven't even been questioned about the torture telegrams. This is sensible - no British jury is going to convict someone for campaigning against government complicity in torture, in support of George Bush. The publicity surrounding a show trial is not something the government would relish.

Which is why it is confusing that the government have decided to prosecute Messrs Keogh and O'Connor for their alleged involvement in the leaking of the memo about George Bush's proposal to bomb al-Jazeera TV.

So why has that prosecution been brought? There are two vital factors.

Firstly, the UK government has little to fear from publicity. It reveals Bush as violent and unbalanced, but we knew that already. From a No 10 point of view, it shows Blair in a good light, talking Bush out of one of his madder schemes. It is evidence that Blair is not just Bush's bitch. This is a message No 10 are keen to get across, so publicity? No problem.

Secondly, the memo was not successfully leaked. If there was indeed an effort to leak it, it was made by people operating in the wrong century. The document wound up at the Daily Mirror, who were too cowardly to publish and tamely gave it back to the government. The days of heroic editors and publishers in the deadwood press are long gone. The mainstream media are completely intimidated by government - especially, let it be said, the BBC.

By contrast, the torture telegrams were featured on over 4,000 blogs worldwide within 72 hours.

Over the al-Jazeera memo the government looks to be

doing the right thing in thwarting bush, and the government looks strong and commanding in suppressing the memo. By contrast, on the torture telegrams, the government has been caught using material from the World's most hideous torture chambers. Jack Straw and Tony Blair have been caught lying about the fact that they do this. And they have been shown to be completely impotent in their efforts to suppress the truth when faced with blogger revolt and modern technology.

They can still try to prosecute me if they want, but WE ARE THE PEOPLE!!

And we cannot be suppressed.

When Moonbats Attack

On 9 January 2006 Channel 4 News published this article by J J King commenting on the release of the classified documents.

Not Leaking, But Blogging

What to do if you can't get your damning documents picked up by the mainstream media? The answer, it seems, is to take it to the blogs-- from whence, if the story has 'legs', it may eventually get dragged into the press.

That is precisely what has happened in the case of Craig Murray, former UK Ambassador to Uzbekistan. Murray lost his position after he defied a Foreign Office prohibition on publishing documents concerning the UK's use of information obtained by rendition and torture (including, incidentally, boiling alive) in the War on Terror.

On Murray's request, bloggers reproduced his documents online, making further suppression practically impossible. The mainstream, now assured that it was not breaking a story that might cause it trouble, ran the Murray story in due course.

The 'Moonbat Craze'

Murray may have a book to promote, but that doesn't make a right wing blogger like Michelle Malkin look any more convincing when she calls the furore around his published telegrams a 'Moonbat Craze'. The documents on offer may not quite be the 'Smoking Gun' Murray claims, but they are certainly significant.

Whereas the Bush regime tacitly condoned torturous methods in February 2002, when it indicated the Geneva Conventions didn't apply to captured members of al Qaeda and Afghanistan's Taliban, the UK had taken no such public stance. In fact, as blog BlairWatch points out, the government has been holding steadfastly, if increasingly unbelievably, to the line that they know nothing about Extraordinary Rendition or torture used to obtain information for the War on Terror.

As a result of Murray's blog publication, such claims now appear 'superlatively disingenuous', as John Lettice puts it for The Register. 'In order to sustain the "see no evil" policy in the face of these,' the telegrams appear to show, Lettice argues, 'Jack Straw must presumably also now claim to have been entirely unaware of what one of his own ambassadors was telling him, repeatedly and at some considerable length.'

Publication of Murder in Samarkand

For 12 months Craig Murray had been putting Murder in Samarkand through the FCO clearance process. He was contractually obliged to clear the manuscript with his former employer.

The FCO had sent out the manuscript to everybody named within it, and the result was several hundred suggested amendments, almost all of which had been accepted. But the FCO was still stalling on giving permission – while directly threatening to prosecute if the book was published.

Murray sent this email ultimatum to the FCO.

To Richard Stagg
Director of Corporate Resources, FCO
7 February 2006
Dickie,
There is now an extensive correspondence over many months on my efforts to clear my book with the FCO for publication. You have had many months to deliberate.
In the ensuing discussions, I have made, as requested, the following very extensive amendments.
*I have removed two accusations that Colin Powell was lying
*I have edited out those parts of my conversation with the US Ambassador which had the quality of confidence, were indiscreet, or differed from public US policy on Uzbekistan
*I have removed the detail of two SIS intelligence reports
*I have removed the reference to GCHQ telephone intercepts
*I have removed completely references to the role of Research Analysts in intelligence analysis

*I have made plain that Duncan does not support my recollection that he said Research Analysts were in tears over pressure brought over claims of Iraqi WMD
*I have changed the attributions of several comments made by Uzbek LE staff
*I have given false names to several Uzbek LE staff
*I have removed several references to my contention that the Embassy did not function well before my arrival
*I have removed the reference to an early hiccough in Andrew Patrick's career
*I have changed statements made by Matthew Kydd and Linda Duffield (frankly, I believe my original account was more accurate)
*I have reduced the gruesome detail of the aircraft crash body identification, and particularly taken out physical detail personal to Richard Conroy
*I have removed or toned down a number of personal observations on FCO staff
*I have taken out the reference to Frank Berman being appointed over David Anderson

I believe the above, which is not exhaustive, is proof of a genuine willingness on my part to compromise to reach agreement. I am deeply disappointed that, throughout this process, I have felt no urge on the part of the FCO to actually conclude this matter. Past correspondence sets out the timescale and the FCO's continued invention of new points to prevent the process concluding.

I therefore give you notice that, should I not receive a definitive response from you by Friday 10 February, I shall be going ahead with publication. In that event I will not feel obliged to retain all the above amendments, some of which I believe detract from the truth of the book and which I offered in response to your various requests, in the belief that we were seeking agreement.

Craig Murray

After receiving a response threatening legal action on three different grounds – defamation, crown copyright and the official secrets act – Murray sent this furious and rather splendid reply.

9 February 2006
Mr Richard Stagg
Director General Corporate Affairs
Foreign & Commonwealth Office
London
Dear Dickie,
Thank you for your letter of 8 February about my forthcoming book, Murder in Samarkand. Let me respond to the points which you have made.

Firstly, allow me to note that, over a period of many months, you have consulted exhaustively with all the FCO staff, past and present, named in the book.

Let me then relate that to the question of libel. In your letter you state that you are 'Also advised that there are a number of passages in your book which could well ground actions for defamation.'

Let me be quite plain. I have no desire to libel or defame anybody. So I urge you now to disclose to me those passages in the book which you have been advised may be defamatory, so that I may consider if I believe there is that danger, and remove or amend any accidental defamation.

I make this offer in all good faith, that we may avoid the publication of defamation. If you choose not to take up this fair offer, and subsequently the FCO or its employees attempt to block publication through court actions for defamation, it will be evident that this is not an attempt to avoid defamation, but a ruse to block publication of the book as a whole through vexatious and unnecessary litigation.

I repeat I have the strongest desire not to defame anybody. I know the terrible mental anguish that unjust defamation can cause. You will recall that I was myself outrageously defamed and accused, quite groundlessly, of appalling things like being an alcoholic and offering visas in exchange for sex. Of course, in my case it was the FCO which was defaming me. The complete story of why and how this happened is in fact the substance of my book. Which is why you are so keen to identify and reserve possible legal avenues for the government to block publication.

It is not falsehood which scares you, but truth.

It is plain from your letter that you object to the whole concept of my publishing this account. Nowhere in the months of negotiation between us to date did you propose any such fundamental objections as now surface in your letter. Rather you asked for a series of specific amendments, the vast majority of which I made. I am sadly reinforced in my view that this lengthy process was an effort on your part to stall publication, rather than a discussion in good faith.

On the specific points you raise, you claim that the publication on my website of material in September caused operational damage to Research Analysts. There has been numerous and frequent correspondence and personal contact between us since September. I am puzzled as to why you mention this now and have not done so before. The material in question featured on my website for 24 hours and has not done so since.

You requested me to remove material from the book which you believed was misleading on the role of Research Analysts and could cause operational difficulty. I immediately removed that passage from the text in its entirety. The only point still at dispute, is that I have in the text that a member of Research Analysts told me that people in that Department were in tears over pressure put on them to go along with claims of Iraqi WMD. You tell me that the officer, still in your employ, now denies telling me this. I have noted in the book that I say he told me this, and he apparently says he did not tell me this. People can draw their own conclusions. I cannot see why this is such a huge problem for you, or would lead you to want to ban a book.

Similarly, I formed a strong impression that the British Embassy in Tashkent was pretty inactive before my arrival. You say that is not your impression. Well, fine. That seems to me well within the range of views that should be able freely to be published in a democracy without political suppression.

I note your point on Crown Copyright. Again, I am genuinely concerned to act in a legal fashion and I should be most grateful if you would explain to me how my book differs from Christopher Meyer's in this regard. You told me that you had personally played a major role within the FCO in supervising the preparation of the 'Dirty Dossier' on Iraqi Weapons of Mass Destruction. I am afraid that one consequence is, that when you try to lecture me on truth, I am sorely tempted to laugh at you. I have lost my livelihood through all this. You have lost something infinitely more precious.

Finally, you threaten me with the Official Secrets Act. I am confident I am not breaking it. And if you really want to ask a jury of twelve honest citizens to send me to prison for campaigning against torture, good luck to you.

Yours Sincerely,
Craig J Murray

The FCO continued to attempt to block publication, writing directly to the publishers. One argument they deployed was that all knowledge Craig Murray had gained in the course of his career belonged to his

employer, the Crown. This article was published on 12 February 2006.

The Foreign and Commonwealth Office seem determined to stop me publishing my book. They are threatening four grounds of legal action:
a) Libel
b) Crown Copyright
c) Breach of Confidence
d) Official Secrets Act

The first point is that plainly this is an attempt to suppress the book and prevent publication by scaring me (and the publishers) with the threat of legal action. This will not work, as neither of us scare easily.

Let us then consider each of these proposed legal actions in turn '

Libel

I am confident that the book is entirely true, and thus does not libel anybody. The FCO is likely nonetheless to try to run a vexatious libel action by one of its staff named in the book. The book cannot be sold in the UK during such action, and this is the most likely way they will attempt to in effect ban the book by using millions of pounds of taxpayers' money in an endless court process

Crown Copyright

Following the publication of Christopher Meyer's book, Jack Straw said that in future the government would actively consider the use of Crown copyright to prevent such further publications. This is a stretching of the copyright law, and the argument goes like this:

When I was in Uzbekistan, I was employed by the Crown, so the intellectual property in anything I learnt belongs to the Crown, just as the copyright of anything created by a Microsoft software designer belongs to Microsoft.

There are three problems in this. First, I don't think my

contract said any of that, while I bet the Microsoft contract does.

The second problem is that they are claiming by book is untrue and inaccurate. They are lying, but that is their claim. If they want to maintain that claim, how can they possibly argues that the Crown has copyright over things which are fictitious and did not happen while I was in their employ? The notion is absurd.

The third problem is much more fundamental. If this applies to me, it would also apply to every other employee of the crown, including not just Christopher Meyer but also, for example, Tony Blair. Now we know that Tony Blair has obtained a huge mortgage on a house based on a guaranteed advance for his memoirs of his time as Prime Minister. Now under the government's new argument, Blair has sold something that didn't belong to him at all, but belonged to the Crown.

The FCO will argue that it is for the Crown Prerogative to decide when to exercise Crown Copyright and when to let it go. In other words, they would sue me and not Tony Blair. And who exercises the Crown Prerogative? Why, the Prime Minister, of course.

So let us be clear about this. By delving about in the most remote and arcane backwaters of Britain's unwritten constitution, the government is seeking to undermine freedom of speech and claim the power arbitrarily to ban books. If this argument were accepted by the courts, the government could ban books under Crown Prerogative without having to give any explanation or reason as to why they decided to ban a 'Dissident' book but allow their own propaganda.

It is essential to fight this completely undemocratic development.

Breach of Confidence

The FCO attempted to frame me with false disciplinary allegations, and leaked the details of those allegations to the press. Plainly they had broken the relationship of confidence between us. Furthermore I believe I am revealing illegal action by the government, breaking both international and domestic law by being complicit in torture.

In these circumstances a 'whistleblower' is protected from this kind of legal harassment. There is no way that the government would win this before the European Court.

Official Secrets Act

This is, of course, the ultimate attempt to scare us by threatening prison against free speech. The large majority of official documents quoted in this book were released to me under the Data Protection Act. There are no other official documents which have not already been released all over the web. I am confident this is bluster ' to ask a jury to convict someone for revealing government malpractice is not sensible, and I would love to see Jack Straw in that witness box.

This is an important fight. We have a government committed to illegal war abroad and an attack across the whole spectrum of civil liberties at home. After banning books comes burning books. If at some stage of the fight they want to send me to prison, I am prepared. We have to show that we will not be cowed, and that the truth cannot be suppressed. Frankly, if the government think they can bury this book, they are even barmier than I thought.

Litigation and Employment Group

Treasury Solicitors
One Kemble Street, London WC2B 4TS

DX 123242 Kingsway
Switchboard: (020) 7210 3000 (GTN 210)
Direct Line: (020) 7210 3393
Direct Fax: (020) 7210 3410
gareth.buttrill@tsol.gsi.gov.uk

Please Quote: LT6/1609F/GXB/1C

Your Reference:

Craig Murray
Flat 1
31 Sinclair Gardens
London
W14 0AU

By courier and by email

7 July 2006

Dear Mr Murray

INFRINGEMENT OF CROWN COPYRIGHT

The Treasury Solicitor acts for the Foreign Secretary in this matter. This letter should be treated as a letter before claim in accordance with the Civil Procedure Rules 1998.

It has come to our attention that, on 4 July 2006, you placed 15 documents on your website (www.craigmurray.co.uk) which you describe as *"supporting documents"* relating to your book 'Murder in Samarkand'. We have reviewed the documents and it is clear that in each case (save for document 12 and the majority of document 13) the copyright in the documents subsists with the Crown. I refer you to section 163(1) of the Copyright, Designs and Patents Act 1988 which states:

"*163(1) Where a work is made by Her Majesty or by an officer or servant of the Crown in the course of his duties –*
(a) the work qualifies for copyright protection notwithstanding section 153(1) (ordinary requirement as to qualification for copyright protection), and
(b) Her Majesty is the first owner of any copyright in the work".

We take the position that all of the documents (save for 12 and the majority of 13) were produced by an officer or servant of the Crown in the course of their duties. As you do not have permission or a licence to reproduce the documents we consider that Crown copyright has been infringed. In particular, you should note that the statement on your website that *"Net posting is not breaching copyright because there is no charge to access the documents"* is wrong as a matter of law. Whether or not a charge is made is wholly irrelevant to the issue of copyright infringement. Further, even if a document is released under the Data Protection Act or Freedom of Information Act that does not entitle you to make further reproductions of that document by, for example, putting them on your website or making further copies to be provided to third parties. The copyright remains enforceable.

As you are infringing Crown copyright, you are required to remove the documents from your website immediately and to provide an undertaking that you will not further infringe Crown

David Dunleavy – Head of Division
Adam Chapman – Team Leader

This attempt to use copyright law, rather than Official Secrets legislation, to suppress leaked documents was unprecedented. Craig Murray found it rather amusing and an opportunity to taunt his former employers. He replied as follows:

To: Gareth Buttrill, Treasury Solicitors
Sent: Friday, July 07, 2006 2:56 PM
Subject: Re: Infringement of Crown Copyright: letter before claim
Mr Buttrill,
As no court has ruled on anything, I would like to know by what power you, acting for the government, can tell me what I "must" do in this respect. I am putting that question formally to you as a government servant and it is not rhetorical; I require an answer.
I find the increasing authoritarianism of government in this country deeply disturbing. I will consider carefully your points once I can get proper legal advice, and not before. It should not take too long.

This brought the following ultimatum by email from Gareth Buttrill:

"We are prepared to extend the deadline for you to give an undertaking until 4pm on Thursday 13 July 2006 on condition that the documents referred to in my first letter are immediately removed from your website and not reproduced by you anywhere else..."

To which Murray, who by now felt sure of his ground, replied like a matador goading a bull:

Mr Buttrill,
Thank you for this second letter. It is rather a peculiar request. You claim to be willing to extend the deadline

for me to be able to take legal advice, providing that I concede the principal point in the meantime.

I cannot see the need for this haste. In copyright cases it is not my understanding that it is generally considered necessary to remove a publication from circulation pending a court decision. For example, there was a recent highly publicised copyright case over the Da Vinci code. Was it deemed necessary by the court to withdraw the Da Vinci Code from sale while the case was heard? No, it was not.

Your peremptory demands reveal the motive behind your actions in this case - the suppression of information for political purposes. I don't believe it is right to use Crown Copyright in this way. Otherwise the government has an arbitrary power to keep secret absolutely anything that it does. Your contention in your letter of 7 July that the government can use Crown Copyright arbitrarily and politically to suppress material released under the Freedom of Information Act, would obviate the whole purpose of that Act in giving the public a "Right to know" what is being done in their name.

I have this morning contacted solicitors to take legal advice. I could not do so over the weekend as this is not a criminal matter, and copyright lawyers do not run 24 hour call out services. Unfortunately I must spend much of today at St Thomas' Hospital for treatment of serious medical conditions. The Foreign & Commonwealth Office's treatment of me, as detailed in the documents you are trying to suppress, was the direct cause of those medical conditions, a fact I would welcome the chance to discuss in court.

You have been free to advise me what I "Must" do. You must bear in mind what the content of the story is, that I am seeking to tell and the government is seeking to suppress.

I accept your renewed deadline as reasonable, but will

not be removing the documents in the interim - until I
get advice, I shall go by what I know of the law, and all I
know in this matter is the Da Vinci Code precedent.
In the meantime, I should be grateful if, entirely without
prejudice, you could furnish me with some practical
advice. If the documents are, as you allege, Crown
Copyright, where and how do I go about making a formal
application for permission to reproduce them?
Also, I am copying your letters to my website. Do you
allege that to be also a breach of Crown Copyright? If I
remove the documents but not your letters, would you
still go for an injunction? If I am served an injunction
and remove the documents, but put the injunction on
my website to explain why, do you allege I am breaching
Crown Copyright by publishing the injunction?
Do you allege it to be a breach of Crown Copyright to
reproduce on a weblog any document at all produced by
government? The definition given in your letter of 7 July
would plainly cover speeches given by Ministers and
written by civil servants. Is it a breach of Crown
Copyright to reproduce such ministerial speeches on a
weblog? How long a quote could you make from a
ministerial speech before breaching copyright? Does this
cover, for example, letters from local authorities and
health trusts, or just from central government? Does it
cover parking tickets? What about quotes from the King
James Bible?
If all or any of these are, in your view, matters of
discretion where the government can exercise Crown
Copyright if it so chooses, then the following is perhaps
the most important question of all. Are there any
criteria of reasonable action which the government is
obliged to consider when deciding whether to enforce
claimed copyright or not, or is the Crown claiming a
power which is solely arbitrary?
I apologise for my confusion. You can see why I need to

take legal advice. I will revert to you.

Craig Murray

Murder In Samarkand Confiscated at Airport Again

From the Guardian 10 September 2006.

The war on terror moves in mysterious ways. Last month, not long after the allegedly planned terrorist attacks on multiple jetliners over the Atlantic were foiled, Ben Paarman turned up at Luton airport for a flight to Berlin. Having forgotten to remove toiletries from his hand luggage, he was hauled over for further inspection, and two books were discovered. A German novel passed without comment, but Murder in Samarkand, Craig Murray's memoir of his incident-strewn stint as British ambassador to Uzbekistan, didn't. "'Is that about terrorism?' asked the lady that examined my onboard luggage," wrote Paarman on neweurasia.net, a collection of blogs by and about Central Asians. "'Humm, well, it contains mentions of that, but it's about your former ambassador to Uzbekistan and more about diplomacy,' I replied politely. 'Does it have al-Qaeda in it?' I looked a bit confused. 'Well, I have to check this with my manager, the rest of your stuff is fine, though.'" The manager arrived, asked Paarman where he got the book (Waterstone's, Islington), then pronounced: "I am afraid you cannot take this onboard, Sir." The book was duly confiscated. This much has already been mentioned, in this paper. But then it happened again.

On Monday Gillian Davison, an actress on her way to New York, reported on the blog that she had had her copy of the same book confiscated at Heathrow. Murray has offered to replace Paarman's copy - and consulted lawyers. "The lawyers said that the first time it might have been just a mistake, not policy," he replied this week, to an email from the Guardian asking how far this course of action had gone, "but twice at two different airports looks like a policy. We are strongly minded to go to the High Court for an injunction under the Human Rights Act."

Political Prosecution
26 April 2007

I was dismissed as Ambassador to Uzbekistan when one of my diplomatic telegrams was leaked to the Sunday Times. The telegram complained of our continual receipt, via the CIA, of intelligence obtained by torture in Uzbekistan. It detailed London meetings which had approved this policy, referred to the CIA flying people to Uzbekistan and handing them over to the Uzbek intelligence services, and explained the illegality of this activity.

Interestingly the Financial Times decided to publish only a tiny fraction of this information, which was explosive back then in October 2003, as extraordinary rendition had not yet hit the headlines. But the leak was enough to get me sacked, and to institute a formal leak inquiry. Once it became plain that I was not the leaker, the inquiry was quietly stopped.

I have therefore been more sensitive than most to the Government's continued habit of leaking "Intelligence" when it suits it. My objection has largely been that the government does this in order to exaggerate the threat of terrorism and instill fear, which they view as helpful in rallying popular support to the "War on Terror".

I was therefore furious when I saw a headline "Al-Qaeda planning Big British Attack" in the Sunday Times of 22 April. So furious I have been carrying the cutting in my pocket all the way to Moscow, until I got the chance to blog about it. I see in the interim the opposition have started making a related point.

The Sunday Times journalist, Dipesh Gadher, claims to have seen a Joint Terrorism Analysis Centre (JTAC) report which justifies the terror stirring headline.

But JTAC reports are almost always Top Secret, and are always classified. Unless Gadher made it all up, he and whoever showed it to him, and his Editor, are all guilty of a serious criminal offence. They should be jailed for many years under the Official Secrets Act.

This is especially true as two gentlemen are currently being tried under precisely that draconian legislation, for possessing the minute of the meeting where George Bush proposed to Tony Blair the bombing of Al-Jazeera TV.

The truth is that both the police and the Crown Prosecution Service act in these matters in a way that is blatantly political. There is no even-handed administration of justice here. If a pro-war antagonist leaks information to whip up public opinion, no action is ever taken. Let me be plain - there is nothing in law that says that secret material can be leaked if it supports the government. Yet they do it all the time.

By what right was David Shayler jailed, but Dipesh Gadher and his informant not even looked at?

Government members and supporters do what they like. But should anyone else follow suit, the full wrath of the Establishment crashes on their head. Even, as in my case, when they didn't actually do it.

The administration of justice is not impartial in the UK.

Abuses By British Troops in Iraq

As the occupation of Iraq dissolved into violence and chaos, public revulsion started to set in both at British losses and at mounting evidence of abuse and atrocities by allied forces. A shocking video of British soldiers beating hooded Iraqi atrocities drew this reflection from Murray who was surprisingly sympathetic to the British soldiers involved.

I feel the need to comment on the video of brutality by British soldiers released at the weekend, purely because so much rubbish has been spouted in the mainstream media on the subject.

I may surprise you by starting with the observation that, on the scale of violence we have visited on Iraq, this was a negligible incident. People on all sides are dying every day. I have heard enough first hand accounts, from British diplomats and military, from journalists and NGO workers that indicate the scale of violence is much worse than the media shows us. Basic services have collapsed. Their world is in chaos, and we should not pretend that the answer to these problems is simply for this group of junior soldiers to be court-martialed.

Actually, I blame them very little. What are they supposed to do to disperse a crowd which, plainly, was trying to inflict actual violence on the troops? If every Iraqi who threw a stone at coalition forces was interned, you would keep millions of prisoners. There are no Iraqi authorities to whom prisoners can be turned over who will deal with them sensibly. The British don't want prisoners, and the UK military now have a de facto policy of not turning prisoners over to the US authorities because of their inept and violent handling of them.

The British troops are in a completely impossible situation. Their role is to support a corrupt and inefficient Iraqi puppet administration which is incapable of exercising control, and would do little for good if it did have control. The vast majority of the Iraqi population do not want us there. The real good that this video might have done is in driving home to the British public, against the ceaseless propaganda of the mainstream media, that we are not wanted. That stone-throwing crowd were Shias, for God's sake. The official propaganda says that they are on 'our' side.

So our troops are being sniped at, blown up or facing violent mobs. They can do little about it. Their own military leadership are convinced that they should not be there. They are not the ones reaping the benefits of huge income from the new US and UK oil contracts, though they will be giving their lives to protect the carpetbaggers who have descended on Iraq like locusts. Is there any wonder that this boils over in frustration?

The disgraceful actions in that video were not the product of intrinsic evil on the part of the British troops involved. This incident was one of the more minor consequences of the illegal war of aggression and occupation launched by George Bush and Tony Blair. It is Blair and Bush, not the troops, who should be in the dock.

Normality and the Jowells

This article of 28 February 2006 represents a widening of focus from just civil liberties and foreign affairs, to a much broader perception of the corruption of the political establishment. The blog was becoming an outlet for stories, or details of stories, which the mainstream media would not publish. Senior cabinet minister Tessa Jowell was caught accepting a payment of £400,000 from Italian PM Sylvia Berlusconi to pay off her mortgage.

Tessa Jowell tells us she did nothing wrong. She merely signed documents to remortgage her home. She strongly asserted today that this was 'a very normal thing to do, and certainly not illegal.'

It is indeed not unusual to remortgage, though it was unusual that she remortgaged with an offshore bank. It is also unusual to remortgage for as much as £400,000. But it is very unusual indeed to remortgage for £400,000, then pay off the full loan, within a month, with spare cash.

What sort of people do such a thing? Well, money launderers. If you have £400,000 of cash not easily explained, you now have remortgage papers available to show where you got it.

Now, where did the money actually come from? Well, on two occasions, David Mills has said in writing that it came from Silvio Berlusconi. He said so in a signed confession to the Italian police, which he now says was extracted under duress. And he said so in a letter to his own accountant, where he explained that it was not in fact a bribe from Berlusconi for the evidence he had just given in an Italian court to keep Berlusconi out of jail. It was rather a personal gift. Mills now says that this second occasion when he wrote that the money came from Berlusconi was in fact a lie to protect another client. One can believe him or not ' he is claiming to be a liar already. What we do know for certain is that, shortly after giving evidence on behalf of Berlusconi, evidence which Italian authorities now allege was perjured, David Mills received a lot of money from an Italian source, which he has difficulty accounting for and claims he needed to disguise. His wife then took out a mortgage for about the same sum, which they almost immediately then paid off again.

It stinks to heaven.

Mills is, beyond dispute, a confidante and adviser of the odious Berlusconi. Mills' job as an international corporate lawyer is to help the cosmopolitan super rich move their money about and avoid tax, and to disguise their cash flows if necessary. Mills is a long term shyster whose activities and profession should appall Labour supporters. Everything Mills stands for is what Keir Hardie and Clement Atlee were against. So it should be of no surprise that he is close to Blair and a member of his personal circle. The day I decided Blair was calculating and self-seeking, rather than honest and misguided, was the day that Blair first chose to spend family holidays with the Berlusconis, at some of their palaces. But Blair's friendship with the likes of Mills should have warned all of us sooner.

Now for something else you won't find in the mainstream media. Mills was under long term surveillance by the Serious Fraud Office for numerous dubious financial transactions. Approximately nine years ago, his office was actually raided by the SFO. As the investigation drew to a close, New Labour came to power. An inside source tells me that SFO staff believed they had a good case, and wondered whether his friendship with the new Prime Minister Blair had any bearing on it not coming to court. A Sunday Times

Insight investigation into Mills was spiked by the editors.

So these current peculiar financial dealings do not drop out of a clear blue sky. A lot of taxpayers' money has been spent investigating Mills before. He is well dodgy.

What will it take for the eyes of the very many decent people still left in the Labour Party to be opened to the appalling people who now lead their party? How many of the current cabinet are not, themselves or their partners, personally millionaires? Blair has a '3 million house. Straw has a Cotswold mansion as one of his homes. We recall Blunkett's dodgy directorships, and Mandelson's loan from Robinson. Who do these people represent, except a self-serving, cosmopolitan elite? Is it any wonder they are so keen on privatising health and education, when they and all their friends can afford the best? And what does any of this have to do with the aims and origins of the Labour Party, or the hopes of those who elected them?

When you have sold your soul to Mammon, you end up doing things like launching illegal wars that kill over a hundred thousand and cost the taxpayer billions, but bring massive profits to your friends who own shares in oil companies or arms manufacturers. I have no doubt that some of those who have made a killing out of the Iraq War will have paid for Mills' useful professional advice on offshore money transactions.

Mills and Blair will be close to those making a killing, but not those suffering the killing. It is hard to see that far from the marble terrace overlooking one of Mr Berlusconi's private beaches.

The next day this article was followed up:

It is a sign of our appalling times, and the arrogance of New Labour, that Blair clings on to his loyal muppet

Jowell, while Sir Gus O'Donnell, Cabinet Secretary, earnestly enquires whether there is anything in the Code of Conduct for Ministers that specifically precludes multiple acts of money laundering.

Well, Sir Gus, there is certainly this; the Code precludes acceptance of gifts. That is what Mills claims this money was. As this "Gift" (note the use of a capital 'G') went to pay off a mortgage which was 50% in Jowell's name and which she had signed, she also accepted it. She should be out. But doubtless the Cabinet Office are working overtime on how to Hutton their way around this one.

In the meantime, the Blairite cheerleaders in the media bravely try to save her. In particular Britain's worst journalist, the wholly odious Michael White (Political editor of the Guardian), argues against all the evidence that Jowell and Mills' finances are separate.

That man White is so far up Jack Straw's rectum that for years he hasn't had any daylight to report by. He also seems not to know that the ministerial code specifically covers gifts to family members.

Two more shockers...

1. Jowell had remortgaged her home to launder money not just once, but five times.

Does she still claim this is "Normal"? On one occasion she had paid it off again in just 19 days.

2. Finally, yesterday I reported a fact that the mainstream media still does not dare to print; that Mills was under Serious Fraud Office investigation (and his office was raided as a result) at around the same time that New Labour came to power. I also reported that some of the SFO staff on the case were confused and concerned that no prosecution arose.

The mainstream press are too scared of this story to tackle it properly, but I'm sure you'll excuse my own caution as I state this next bit very, very carefully:

I have seen no evidence to suggest to me that it was a

particular handicap to Mr Mills at around that time that his sister-in-law, Barbara Mills, was the Director of Public Prosecutions and a former Head of the Serious Fraud Office.

I mean no more than appears on the face of that sentence.

On 2nd March 2007 he returned to the subject:

"Sir Gus O'Whitewash has ruled. Tessa Jowell did not break the rules because for four years David Mills did not tell her he had received what he then believed was a gift of $600,000.

How nice it must be to be so fabulously wealthy that a gift of $600,000 is so unimportant to you that you do not even bother to mention it to your partner!

Actually, I have a lot of experience of the very rich, and they are much more obsessed with money than the poor, and certainly talk about it more. I just don't believe Jowell.

This is particularly true as the money was used to pay off a large remortgage which she herself had just taken out. She is now saying that she didn't have any idea, or apparently ask, where all the money to pay off the mortgage came from.

There is also a peculiar bit of reasoning by Sir Gus O'Whitewash. Jowell alleges that she did not know about the money for four years, and by that time tax was paid for it, so it had become earnings, not a gift.

Actually, that doesn't follow. If you receive a large cash gift it is still classed as income, and taxable.

Of course, what we still do not know, is who this money came from, and why. If it did not come from Berlusconi or from another illegitimate source, show us the paper trail. It is inconceivable that such a large sum from any legitimate source is not documented.

That money was used to pay off a mortgage which was 50% in Jowell's name. So to accept it is only her husband's business is simply nonsense.

Whitehall's whitewash has become so watery as to cover up nothing.

By the next day indignation had reached new heights:

I now learn that Tessa Jowell not only claims that she did not know that her husband had received $600,000, but did not know that her own mortgage had been paid off.

I simply do not believe her. Let me be perfectly plain. I am calling her a liar. Go on, sue me.

I recently paid off my mortgage. That involves paperwork. It also involves the deeds of the house being sent from the mortgage company. This is a very careful and important transaction, and the mortgage company will make absolutely certain that it has the agreement of all parties to the mortgage as to where the deeds are being sent. Paying off a mortgage in your name is simply not the sort of thing you can miss happening.

Presumably she also didn't notice for four years she wasn't receiving any mortgage statements.

Who does believe her? I should be most grateful if anyone who does believe her could sign in and leave a comment. In fact, please sign in and tell me whatever you think. (I am sorry about the signing in, but it isn't painful and has reduced the porno spam in which we would otherwise be drowning).

One last thought. If you do believe her, do you think that a woman who does not know if her own home is mortgaged or not, who does not know her family income within the odd 600 thousand dollars or so, is a sensible person to put in charge of an Olympic Games?

The Guardian Leader the following day marked a break with that newspaper, for which he had been writing fairly regularly:

The Guardian's editor Alan Rusbridger still tries to defend his personal friend Tessa Jowell. From today's Guardian Leader:
"Ms Jowell has been acquitted by a questionable procedure. That does not make her guilty; a less questionable procedure would very likely acquit her too."
Oh yes. A genuinely independent judge would have no difficulty believing that her husband did not tell her for four years that he received a $600,000 gift, or that she saw nothing to indicate the mortgage had been paid off. Or that when she then remortgaged the same house again - twice - it did not occur to her that this would not be a problem if, as she claims, she believed the first mortgage had not been paid off.
Let me rephrase my "Does anyone believe her?" question. Does anyone believe her except Alan Rusbridger and Michael White? We all wait for Polly Toynbee's article entitled "Money laundering is OK if you have a peg on your nose."
(I suppose I ought to explain that. At the last general election, Polly Toynbee's Guardian column urged voters to vote New Labour but to show their disapproval of the illegal war on Iraq by wearing a peg on their nose while they did it.)

Having claimed she had no idea who was paying her joint mortgage, and effectively disowned her husband, Jowell announced a separation from him – which proved to be as phoney as Craig Murray here predicted.
The latest move in the Jowell scandal is the most cynical

bit of media manipulation. Tearful Tessa, lower lip trembling, eyes welling, torn apart from the man she loves. Altogether now: Aaah! But wait - there is hope. The couple need time to "rebuild" their relationship. So they will get back together after all, in a happy reconciliation, probably just after the local elections.

Who could be so stupid as to buy this crap? Well, the BBC has been reporting it all morning without the tiniest touch of irony. Even the saintly Martin Bell was wheeled out to say that Tessa is now out of the woods.

This answers none of the questions about the money laundering and the corrupt payment she has already received, and is plainly a ploy to divert attention from the continual lies she has told about her involvement in the family finances. Her story yesterday wouldn't stand up to a moment's genuine scrutiny - so let's divert the scrutiny.

It is as if Fred and Rosemary West had said: "OK, we've separated now. We'll see if we can rebuild our relationship. So there is no longer any need to dig up the garden or the cellar."

The Jowell affair had a major impact on the development of Craig Murray's world view. It crystallised his thoughts on the corruption of the Establishment and on its solidarity in defending itself, including through its corrupt media acolytes. This observation is from 5 March 2006.

Sky News has a viewers' vote which shows 88% believe that Tessa Jowell should resign. However they have two guests to discuss the issue with Adam Boulton. One was her friend and former ministerial colleague Baroness Jay and the other her junior minister! They are featuring nobody who thinks she should resign.

The BBC is still worse. The streamer under BBC News 24

regularly tells us that the separation is not a ploy to save her political career. I listened to Radio 4, watched Andrew Marr's political programme and BBC New 24 from 9.55 to 10.40. Not a single critic of Jowell has appeared on the BBC, even though it is the headline story on all these outlets. They are simply deluging us with pro-Jowell propaganda.

For anyone who ever doubted the existence of the "Establishment", this is a real lesson. The views of the people can't get on to the media at all.

Lecture to Massachusetts Institute of Technology
20 May 2006

Thank you. Thank you very much. Good evening ladies and gentlemen. I am delighted to be here in the United States. I agree wholeheartedly with Larry's point that it's very, very necessary to radicalize the current generation of students. I'm not quite sure about the means - that, you know, we need to radicalize the students. Let's find an upper class retired ambassador and send him on a speaking tour. It's not automatically the way I would do it. But we will give it a go and see what happens.

I've never been to Boston before except for Boston in England and I'd never been in the Massachusetts Institute of Technology before. I'm dead impressed by this facility. From here I can see two different clocks and one of them is only about 20 metres east of the other. And yet the technology can detect that it is eight o'clock over there. They are still seven fifty nine over there. I tell you I'm bloody impressed. Quite remarkable.

I was the British ambassador in a place called Uzbekistan. This came at the rather premature end of my diplomatic career. I'd been a career diplomat for 21 years. I served in a number of positions including some senior positions. I was also an expert in Iraqi weapons procurement. Having led the British effort on managing Iraqi attempts at weapons procurement during the early 1990s and during the first Gulf War I was posted to Uzbekistan, and I didn't have that much idea where it was at the time I was posted there.

In fact I was British Deputy High Commissioner in Africa, in Ghana, in Accra. I received a phone call from the office. "Craig you've been promoted to ambassador". And I said "Great". They said "In Uzbekistan" and I said

"Yes". And I put down the phone and I shouted to my secretary "Wendy, go buy an atlas". To see where I was going.

To a wonderful place. Immediately north of Afghanistan, it contains some incredible historic cities like Bokhara and Samarkand. The place where actually Alexander the Great. reigned for two years. This is where he married Roxanne. He actually stayed for two years, longer in one place here than he stayed anywhere else. Where Omar Khayyam wrote the Rubaiyat. It's got a wonderful history to it. It's a place where algebra was invented, so it's had some bad times as well.

And now it's having some of its worst times. It was part of the Soviet Union and I think I need to explain something of that place. It's reckoned by Amnesty International by Freedom House by Human Rights Watch to be among the five worst despotisms on earth. In the same category as North Korea and Burma. It is awful. It's an absolutely totalitarian dictatorship of a Stalinist kind. The people who are in charge are precisely the same people who were in charge during the Soviet Union. President Islam Karimov was President of the Uzbek Soviet Socialist Republic. The Soviet system has essentially stayed in place. We have an added level of brutality and an even greater level of corruption. There's no freedom of speech at all. There's no independent media at all. Opposition is not allowed at all. No elections in which we opposition can compete. There's no freedom of religion.

It's hard to be certain but there are at least 10,000 political and religious prisoners and torture is practiced on a widespread scale, on an industrial scale. Thousands of people are subjected to torture. Eventually I will come on to more detail on that but I also want to tell you something the economy. It's the world's second largest exporter of cotton. Undoubtedly, at least a quarter of you in this hall are likely to have Uzbek cotton in the garments you are wearing. You won't know that, because your garments tell you where they're made. They don't tell you where the cotton came from.

The Uzbek population, 60 percent of them live on state farms. Cotton production and cotton trading is a government monopoly. The people who live on those state farms are slaves. Cotton slaves. They don't only still have the Soviet system of exit visas. They have a system of internal visas. If you want to move from one village to another village you need a visa and if you're a cotton worker you won't get it. Because you're needed on the farms to pick the cotton. 95 percent of it is picked by hand; cotton workers work 12 hours a day, six days a week, and they are paid two dollars a month - two dollars a month. Which they don't always get.

So here you have a brutal dictatorship. Which is noted but it's persecution of all religions. Most of the religious prisoners are Islamic, but they include Jehovah's Witnesses. They include Baptists, there are lot of Baptists in Uzbek prisons. So you have essentially a Communist Government there oppressing its people. And persecuting Baptists. And that doesn't sound automatically like a good ally for George Bush, does it? But it was.

In that period I was there, from August 2002 to October of 2004, Uzbekistan was a close ally of the United States. In 2002 alone, you the American taxpayers gave 500 million dollars in aid to the Karimov regime. And if I can give you a comparison; that's more than you gave to West Africa. You gave 500 million dollars to the Karimov regime of which 120 million dollars was in military aid, basically military equipment for the Uzbek army, and 80 million dollars was to the Uzbek security services the people who do the torture.

Now you might wonder why. Why was America doing

this? Well I'm going to read you a letter. It's an interesting letter. It is dated the 3rd of April 1997 and it's addressed to the honorable George W. Bush, Governor of the state of Texas. And it's from an interesting man, Kenneth L. Lay chairman and chief executive officer of Enron. A gentleman who I should say has never been convicted of anything - yet. And it reads as follows.

"Dear George" it says. It originally said "Dear Governor Bush" but Ken Lay – who George Bush now claims he hardly knew – crossed out "Governor Bush" and inserted "Dear George", "you'll be meeting with Ambassador Sadiq Safayev. Uzbekistan's ambassador to the United States on April 8th. Ambassador Safayev has been finance minister and the senior adviser to President Karimov before assuming his nation's most significant foreign responsibility. Enron has established an office in Tashkent. And we are negotiating a two billion dollar joint venture with Neftigaz Uzbekistan and Gazprom of Russia to develop Uzbekistan's natural gas and transport it to markets in Europe, Kazakhstan and Turkey. This project can bring significant economic opportunities to Texas as well as to Uzbekistan".

That's particularly to one individual in Texas.

"The political benefits to the United States and to Uzbekistan are important to that entire region. I know you and Ambassador Safayev will have a productive meeting which will result in a friendship between Texas and Uzbekistan."

And that meeting happened. Governor Bush met the ambassador with an Enron representative's presence at that meeting, and they agreed this deal for Enron to develop Uzbek gas fields. So at that time while Governor Bush was governor of Texas, the policy of United States of America was not to have anything to do with Uzbekistan because of its appalling human rights record. Madeleine Albright made a very strong speech condemning the human rights record of Uzbekistan. But Governor Bush was developing his own alternative foreign policy and once the Bush administration came into power relations with Uzbekistan warmed up enormously. And that was before September 11th.

After September the 11th the United States moved in and after an agreement with President Karimov established a military base in Uzbekistan in the town of Karshi where three squadrons of the United States Air Force were stationed and a population of U.S. Marines that was normally over 3000 U.S. Marines. So a large United States Air Base, and also the CIA moved in and it became a key U.S. interest to keep President Karimov in power, and keep any dissidents or opponents down.

Now then Uzbeks are human beings like you and me they no more want to be slaves on a cotton farm than you or I do. They value freedom of speech, they would value the opportunity to dissent as much as you or I. Some of them try to do it. What happens to them?

They try. They are clapped into jail immediately and they are tortured. When I say torture, I am not talking about definitions and "does it count as torture if you are deprived of sleep for a couple of days", which I think it does. But we're not talking about that. I had been ambassador for about three weeks when photographs appeared on my desk which had been sent to me by an old Uzbek lady, Fatima Akhmedova. She had been presented with the body of her son in a casket.

He had been in Jaslik, an old Soviet gulag in the middle of the Kizyl Kum desert. She was ordered to bury the casket the next day, not to open the casket, and a guard was set on the casket. He fell asleep in the middle of the night and this extraordinary lady managed to get the casket open, and get the heavy body of her son out onto the kitchen table and take detailed photographs which she sent to me. I sent them on to the pathology laboratory of the University of Glasgow. I've received a report based on the photographs which said that the gentleman's fingernails had been ripped out. He had been severely beaten about the face and he had died of immersion in boiling liquid.

It was immersion not splashing, because there was a tide mark around his upper torso and upper limbs. And when people talk of torture and complicity worldwide of the United States administration in torture, that's what you're talking about. That's what torture is. It's not some hypothetical clean thing. It's vicious. It's disgusting.

Let me explain to you why I talk of the complicity of United States administration and the British administration. I was seeing a stream of intelligence material which came from the CIA. There was a very large CIA station in Tashkent. There was actually no MI6 station in Tashkent. It was too dangerous for MI6, forget James Bond. That's a myth. They don't go dangerous places. No MI6 officer has ever been to any city where you can't buy a cappuccino.

But the CIA, to be fair, were there in great numbers and closely linked. Now remember the Uzbek security services who boiled that guy to death in 2002 alone received over 80 million dollars from the American taxpayer. You guys heated the water. The CIA were presenting this regular stream of intelligence material and at first I found it puzzling. As time went on I understood it, and what the intelligence material was saying was that any dissident in Uzbekistan, any opposition figure, was a member of al-Qaida was an Islamic militant, and very often very often the material said specifically that this named Uzbek opposition member was a member of al-Qaida and had traveled to Afghanistan and met Osama bin Laden. I saw this stuff so often but I was really amazed because this was 2002 in which time Osama bin Laden was presumed hiding. And yet he was able to see all these scores of visitors from Uzbekistan who seemed to have no difficulty finding him. This gave me some reason to doubt the validity of this CIA intelligence. I doubted it even more when one Uzbek opposition figure was named as a member of al-Qaida, when I knew he was a Jehovah's Witness. There are very few Jehovah's Witnesses in al-Qaida.

What the hell is going on? Why is the CIA sending this stuff? There was more - there was CIA material about an al-Qaida training camp in the hills above Samarkand and from which the terrorists were going to swoop down and annex the city of Samarkand. But we knew the location. We had been - my defence section had been to the specified location and there was nothing there.

The CIA who had 20 times as many staff as I did could find there was nothing there. Why were they feeding this false intelligence? I started reporting back to London: "This is false intelligence."

I should explain something to you of the background to this which is the UK/US intelligence sharing agreement, founded by Roosevelt and Churchill during the Second World War. A very good agreement which was much needed at the time. The UK and the US share all our intelligence. The CIA and MI6 share everything, as do NSA and GCHQ Which is our listening station. Share everything. So I was receiving these CIA reports as a customer. Just as people in the administration in Washington would be receiving them. And just as British ministers would be receiving them.

So I would see exactly what Colin Powell or Condoleezza Rice would see if it was an important enough report to reach up to that level. And most reports of Osama Bin Laden they did reach up to that level and these reports said something else. They all said that they were from detainee debriefing by a friendly intelligence agency. By that they met the Uzbek security services and I knew by now the methods of the Uzbek security service. I was meeting people who had been tortured themselves. I saw the physical evidence of torture on their bodies. I saw photographs of people who had been tortured. I spoke to the families of people who had been tortured. I had letters from people who have been tortured, smuggled out of jails. And I was learning what the people who had been tortured were being forced to sign up to. And guess what. The stories they were being forced to sign up to were identical to the stories which were turning up in the CIA intelligence reports.

They were being made to sign to say that they knew that this or that opposition guy was a member of Al-Qaida and had been to Afghanistan and seen Osama bin Laden. Often they were being made to sign to say that people who they had never heard of were members of al-Qaida. I met an old man whose children had been tortured in front of him until he signed something to say his two nephews were members of al-Qaida. And the truth is if you torture someone's children in front of them, they will sign anything. There's almost nobody in this whole world who wouldn't sign anything if you torture their children in front of them. And the CIA is prepared to accept material got by that kind of method.

Now what kind of bloody state have we come to when we have fallen to that level of depravity in pursuit of this so-called war on terror? It is we who are fostering the Taliban now.

But why do it? Now the material is false. Why do it? Well it's exactly what Scott Ritter said. You know all the material on weapons of mass destruction was false. We had a British government which produced that dossier of the intelligence and of course what isn't often said is this: I've just told you about intelligence sharing. Most of it was actually American source not ours, but we produced the dossier because that was felt to be a better public relations thing for the United Nations, that it came from the British not from the US. A dossier of weapons of mass destruction containing 38 key facts, every single one of which turned out to be a lie.

But it was useful. They found the intelligence useful because it justified the war. And equally, they found the false intelligence on Uzbekistan useful because they could say all these people who wanted democracy in Uzbekistan, they didn't want democracy they were actually Al Qaida. That justified all the money being given to President Karimov. And the purpose of that was the Enron oil and gas contract.

And ask yourself this. Nowadays of course they say it wasn't for WMD it's about democracy. So you go to war for democracy in Iraq and at the same time you're paying hundreds of millions of dollars to stop democracy in Uzbekistan. Where is the logic? Whereas the true answer of course has nothing to do with democracy. It's about oil and gas and you go to war to get the oil and gas in Iraq and you pay a dictator to get the oil and gas in Uzbekistan. And that's the naked truth behind the policies of the current U.S. administration,which to my huge shame are simply followed by the United Kingdom government.

I protested back to London. Before I protested, I asked my deputy to call at the American embassy and say to them "My ambassador is extremely worried. He believes the CIA material is coming from torture by the Uzbek authorities. He's going to protest London. Do you have anything in place to make sure this material doesn't come from torture?"

I didn't want to make a fool of myself by protesting if there was going to be an easy answer. The American embassy replied to her "yes, it probably does come from torture but we don't see that as a problem in the context of a war on terror." And I want to be absolutely plain to you. The CIA knew everything I have just told you. They knew how intelligence was gotten. Why did they want it if it wasn't true? They wanted to justify the policy was there. To benefit specific American commercial interests.

The irony of all this is it didn't work. One thing history should tell us; it's not that long ago since the United States was funding and backing Osama bin Laden. They funded him in Afghanistan. I had friends who were actually fighting him on the Soviet side. At that time we also backed and funded Saddam Hussein. It was specifically Donald Rumsfeld and Dick Cheney who started off the Iranian nuclear program. And the truth is that when you back dodgy dictatorships you're always going to get your hand bitten.

And after Enron collapsed, President Karimov had taken a large bribe from Enron. So the deal's off, Enron's collapsed. The Americans tried to persuade him to go with Texaco or Exxon instead. And he said "No, get lost! I'm going with Gazprom because I got 88 million dollars for them. I got paid twice which was very good."

The American base got kicked out and Bush lost. So you lost a billion dollars of American money. You lost a great deal of integrity and you got nothing out of it in the end. And that's part of the problem. The policy is stupid and it's no way of fighting terrorism. There was virtually nobody in Uzbekistan who was anti-American before 2000. Virtually nobody. After three years of solid American support for that dictatorship a huge number of people in Uzbekistan hate the United States. And that's because of George W. Bush. And that's true all over the world.

In 2001. The total membership of al-Qaida Worldwide was probably about 800 people maximum. Minimum 300. Somewhere between them; intelligence analysis is not an exact science but 800 maximum.

Now according to the U.S. military there's 30,000 just in Iraq. How are we winning the war on terror where we are causing hatred which multiplies it? I'm not a violent man. I'm not a militarist but I tell you something. If someone took my brother and boiled him to death I would get a gun and go and try and shoot someone. It's a natural reaction. I'm sorry.

We talk about the insurgency in Iraq and just look at the words being used here. What does the word insurgent mean? It means someone who surges in. No, the Iraqis were there in the first place so they are not insurgents, are they? We are. We've surged into their country and invaded them. Then when they protest about it, we have the cheek to call them insurgents.

It's counterproductive. We are not winning the war on terror. And we are obviating the system of international law. When I protested to London, I was told that we were not breaking the terms of the United Nations Convention Against Torture because we were not doing the torturing ourselves. Nor had we specifically requested that the named individual be tortured. and they said as long as that's the case, we're in the clear, it's legal. And that's the legal advice on which the British government and the U.S. government proceed.

And when you get that bit of intelligence from the CIA, the CIA had removed the name before they issue a report; you don't have the name of the man who was "debriefed". You don't have the detainee, it doesn't tell you his name but just tells you the information. That name's removed on purpose so you can't check if he was tortured or not. And that enables Condoleezza Rice to say, as she has said as she said when she was questioned before the Council of Europe, "I have never knowingly seen intelligence obtained by torture." Because it's deliberately sanitized on the way up to her to give that deniability. But the deniability is lies. There's a structure of lies on which this whole war on terror is based. And on the basis of this material obtained by lies they continually tell us about an ever expanding terror threat. To try to terrorize *us* into complicity they get some poor guy, they torture him into saying he or someone else is a terrorist. And that guy will be detained without trial, to keep the truth well hidden.

We are losing our civil rights. We are losing our moral values. We are losing the fabric of international law and we are creating a hatred for ourselves in the Islamic world which will last our lifetimes even if we stop now.

We have to fight it. Ladies and gentlemen this goes to the banality of evil. The people I worked with they all supported me. You know I'd been in the service for 20 years or so. They said "You're a brave man you're doing a great thing. We support you. I wouldn't stick my neck out like that." And they wouldn't, because they want to keep their jobs. They're not bad people. But all this torture material is being processed by British ambassadors in Egypt, in Saudi Arabia, by my replacement in Uzbekistan, in Morocco, in Syria.

The CIA people, the American ambassadors, American diplomats, hundreds of people in total are involved in this. But it's exactly the fact that in WW2 hundreds and thousands of ordinary Germans were involved in sending people to ashpits. And it wasn't that they were individually evil. The truth is we are on a kind of path where we don't respect individuals, where we demonize a minority, we demonize Islam, we say "but Muslims are a danger who are going to blow us all up and they have to be controlled, and have to be detained without trial and they can be tortured, and they shouldn't have human rights." And honestly I believe that we are on the start of the path that leads towards fascism.

And history shows that you have to stop it.

Because if you don't stop it at the start, you very soon

find it is too late and you have lost your ability to do something about it. So I ask you those of you haven't been much involved, make today the day you wake up. Realize what's happening and you pledge yourselves to work to stop it. It does not have to be this way.

Thank you.

The Famous Liquid Bomb Plot

Craig Murray was – and remains – highly sceptical about the official narrative of the "liquid bomb plot" that led to the extraordinary increase in air passenger checks – which he regards as "Theatre of Security" designed to inculcate the atmosphere that enables government authoritarianism.
This from 14 August 2006.

I have been reading very carefully through all the Sunday newspapers to try and analyse the truth from all the scores of pages claiming to detail the so-called bomb plot. Unlike the great herd of so-called security experts doing the media analysis, I have the advantage of having had the very highest security clearances myself, having done a huge amount of professional intelligence analysis, and having been inside the spin machine.
So this, I believe, is the true story.
None of the alleged terrorists had made a bomb. None had bought a plane ticket. Many did not even have passports, which given the efficiency of the UK Passport Agency would mean they couldn't be a plane bomber for quite some time.
In the absence of bombs and airline tickets, and in many cases passports, it could be pretty difficult to convince a jury beyond reasonable doubt that individuals intended to go through with suicide bombings, whatever rash stuff they may have bragged in internet chat rooms.
What is more, many of those arrested had been under surveillance for over a year - like thousands of other British Muslims. And not just Muslims. Like me.
Nothing from that surveillance had indicated the need for early arrests.
Then an interrogation in Pakistan revealed the details of this amazing plot to blow up multiple planes - which,

rather extraordinarily, had not turned up in a year of surveillance. Of course, the interrogators of the Pakistani dictator have their ways of making people sing like canaries. As I witnessed in Uzbekistan, you can get the most extraordinary information this way. Trouble is it always tends to give the interrogators all they might want, and more, in a desperate effort to stop or avert torture. What it doesn't give is the truth.

The gentleman being "interrogated" had fled the UK after being wanted for questioning over the murder of his uncle some years ago. That might be felt to cast some doubt on his reliability. It might also be felt that factors other than political ones might be at play within these relationships. Much is also being made of large transfers of money outside the formal economy. Not in fact too unusual in the British Muslim community, but if this activity is criminal, there are many possibilities that have nothing to do with terrorism.

We then have the extraordinary question of Bush and Blair discussing the possible arrests over the weekend. Why? I think the answer to that is plain. Both in desperate domestic political trouble, they longed for "Another 9/11". The intelligence from Pakistan, however dodgy, gave them a new 9/11 they could sell to the media. The media has bought, wholesale, all the rubbish they have been shoveled

We then have the appalling political propaganda of John Reid, Home Secretary, making a speech warning us all of the dreadful evil threatening us and complaining that "Some people don't get" the need to abandon all our traditional liberties. He then went on, according to his own propaganda machine, to stay up all night and minutely direct the arrests. There could be no clearer evidence that our Police are now just a political tool. Like all the best nasty regimes, the knock on the door came in the middle of the night, at 2.30am. Those arrested included a mother with a six week old baby. For those who don't know, it is worth introducing Reid. A hardened Stalinist with a long term reputation for personal violence, at Stirling University he was the Communist Party's "Enforcer", (in days when the Communist Party ran Stirling University Students' Union, which it should not be forgotten was a business with a very substantial cash turnover). Reid was sent to beat up those who deviated from the Party line.

We will now never know if any of those arrested would have gone on to make a bomb or buy a plane ticket. Most of them do not fit the "Loner" profile you would expect - a tiny percentage of suicide bombers have happy marriages and young children. As they were all under surveillance, and certainly would have been on airport watch lists, there could have been little danger in letting them proceed closer to maturity - that is certainly what we would have done with the IRA.

In all of this, the one thing of which I am certain is that the timing is deeply political. This is more propaganda than plot. Of the over one thousand British Muslims arrested under anti-terrorist legislation, only twelve per cent are ever charged with anything. That is simply harassment of Muslims on an appalling scale. Of those charged, 80% are acquitted. Most of the very few - just over two per cent of arrests - who are convicted, are not convicted of anything to do terrorism, but of some minor offence the Police happened upon while trawling through the wreck of the lives they had shattered.

Be sceptical. Be very, very sceptical.

He followed this up on 17 August 2006

I appear to have hit a nerve with my call for a sceptical view of the alleged "bigger than 9/11" plot. Over 50,000 people so far have read the item on my own blog, and it has been quoted and reposted all over the web.

In the UK, at least, the more serious wing of the mainstream media is beginning to catch up with the idea that all is not well here.

Still, after eight days of detention, nobody has been charged with any crime. For there to be no clear evidence yet on something that was "imminent" and "Mass murder on an unbelievable scale" is, to say the least, rather peculiar. The 24th person, who was arrested amid much fanfare yesterday, has been quietly released without charge today. Breaking news, another "suspect" has just been released too.

The drip, drip of information to the media from the security services has rather dried-up. The last item of any significance was that they had found a handgun and a rifle - neither of which could have been in any use in the alleged plot. If you were smuggling undetectable liquid explosive onto a plane, you would be unlikely to give the game away by tucking a rifle into your hand baggage.

As with the murder some years ago of the uncle of the suspect held in Pakistan, it remains a possibility that there could be some criminal activity here involving a few of the suspects, which is not terrorist linked.

As the Police immediately told the press about the guns, it is a reasonable deduction that it remains true that they still have found no bombs or detonators, or they would have told us, particularly as they haven't charged anyone yet. They must be getting pretty desperate to announce some actual evidence by now.

This brings us to one particularly sinister aspect of the allegations - that the bombs were to be made on the plane.

The idea that high explosive can be made quickly in a plane toilet by mixing at room temperature some nail polish remover, bleach, and Red Bull and giving it a quick stir, is nonsense. Yes, liquid explosives exist and are highly dangerous and yes, airports are ill equipped to detect them at present. Yes, it is true they have been used on planes before by terrorists. But can they be quickly manufactured on the plane? No.

The sinister aspect is not that this is a real new threat. It is that the allegation may have been concocted in order to prepare us for arresting people without any actual bombs.

Let me fess up here. I have just checked, and our flat contains nail polish remover, sports drinks, and a variety of household cleaning products. Also MP3 players and mobile phones. So the authorities could announce - as they have whispered to the media in this case - that potential ingredients of a liquid bomb, and potential timing devices, have been discovered. It rather lowers the bar, doesn't it?

This has a peculiar resonance for me. I spoke at the annual Stop the War conference a couple of months ago. I referred to the famous ricin plot. For those outside the UK, this generated the same degree of hype here two years ago. It was alleged that a flat in North London inhabited by Muslims was a "Ricin" factory, manufacturing the deadly toxin which could kill "hundreds of thousands of people". Police tipped off the authorities that traces of ricin had been discovered. In the end, all those accused were found not guilty by the court. The "traces of ricin" were revealed to be the atmospheric norm.

The "intelligence" on that plot had been extracted under torture in Algeria - another echo here, as the "intelligence" in this current case has almost certainly been extracted under torture in Pakistan. Another police tip-off to the media was that the intelligence said that the ricin had been stored in plastic jars, and they had indeed found plastic jars containing a suspicious substance. It turned out the containers in question were two Brylcreem tubs. What was in them? In the first, paper clips. In the second, Brylcreem.

I told the story in my speech, and concluded with a ringing "So we must congratulate the government for saving us from a dastardly Islamic plot to take over the World using hair styling products."

I fear the government may have taken me seriously!

I do not discount the possibility that there is a germ of something behind the current alleged plot. Will it be anything like the hype? No.

The hype scarcely lowers. On the flagship ten o'clock news last night, the BBC reported breathlessly on the United flight diverted from Washington to Boston last night, and its fighter escort. We had very earnest besuited security experts terrifying us about the dangers.

The extraordinary thing was that, by this stage, we knew definitely that this was a 60 year old woman with claustrophobia, who had a few loose matches and some Vaseline intensive care hand lotion in the bottom of her handbag. The facts reported were totally at odds with the whole manner of the "be terrified" report and the analysis being built on it. But that didn't stop them.

It has, of course, worked. When did you last see Iraq on the news? Where is Liebermann's defeat now on the news agenda?

A blog like this is much too small a player to affect the public mood. What it can do is tap into it. The extraordinary response to these posts shows that there is a very significant section of the public not prepared to buy more Bush/Blair propaganda.

And again the following day

One aspect of the alleged bomb plot which has provided a tremendous boost to the atavists, is the so-called "Baby bottle bomb".

As the Daily Telegraph reported on August 14, "Scotland Yard are quizzing Abdula Ahmed, 25, and his 23 year old wife Cossor over suspicions that they were to use their baby's bottle to hide a liquid bomb".

This appalling and macabre idea is just what the rabid right needed to stoke up images of how sub-human Muslims are. Prepared to blow up their own baby! For example, John Howard, Australian Prime Minister:

"That would be an appalling reflection on the lack of humanity of that child's parents."

That is one of the more moderate quotes. I won't repeat some of the stuff from US blogs.

One allegation on those blogs, that I can't track down any original source for, is that the police found baby bottles containing residues of potentially bomb-making chemicals. This allegation has also been quoted to me in comments on this website.

Whether police really have said this, is a matter I can't clarify. But if they have, consider this. I am looking at a bottle of Milton sterilising tablets. I, and generations of British parents, used these or similar chemicals to sterilise my baby's feeding bottle. The instructions read thus:

Active Ingredient

Sodium Dichloroisocyanurate

Warnings

Harmful if swallowed. When in contact with an acid, releases a toxic gas.

Hydrogen peroxide is also widely sold in pharmacists and can be used for various domestic purposes including as a disinfectant.

A very high proportion of baby bottles would show traces of potentially dangerous chemicals. It means nothing.

I hope that the allegation is untrue and this young family

intended no such crime. But there is nothing uniquely Islamic about infanticide. Indeed, in the last two days the news bulletins have covered prominently the stories of a British man who allegedly jumped from a balcony clutching his two children in Crete, and the inquest on a woman who threw herself under her train with her nine year old child.

Horrible? Yes. Have Muslims wreaked more horror on the World, either historically or in the last five years, than those professing other religions? No.

The Association of Chief Police Officers reacted against Craig Murray's views about the liquid bomb plot, and this exchange of letters appeared in The Guardian:

Saturday August 19, 2006
By Chief Constable Ken Jones
President, Association of Chief Police Officers

Craig Murray has a lot to say about something of which he knows very little (The timing is political, August 18). The police service in this country is wholly independent of politics and the government. His suggestion that the arrests we saw last week were politically motivated is wholly false. As a one-time senior diplomat, he ought to have a better understanding of the constitutional framework within which policing operates in the UK.

The police service acts solely in the public interest against individuals or groups about whom there is reasonable suspicion or intelligence that they may be engaged in criminal acts. Those criminal acts sometimes include terrorism. The police service does not target or "criminalise" any part of any community. The suggestion that this operation was timed to generate some sort of political benefit is nonsense. The independent decision to act was made in order to ensure the public were protected. Murray must know that high-level liaison between nations facing these challenges is desirable. We are facing an ideologically motivated global threat which demands a united global response.

The police service does not "harass" any religious group. Senior police officers have questioned calls to crudely profile travelers and are leading much of the work to ensure that no one community is victimised. But there is a tiny number of people who, by distorting the core messages of Islam, pose a large-scale threat to us all. We brief our staff very carefully around issues of race, ethnicity, cultures and religions to ensure that dangerous stereotyping does not influence our actions.

We carefully assess the nature of the threat and put into place measures that will contest it. Letting terrorist operations "proceed closer to maturity" could mean that hundreds, or even thousands, might die. It seems we are damned if we act and will most certainly be damned for all time if we do not. Let us remember that those detained last week are innocent until proven guilty. We now need to give the investigators, who are police officers and staff from across the UK, the time and space to establish the truth.

Finally, global terrorism investigations are extremely complex. They involve inquiries across a number of nations. To see no charges after only seven days is hardly surprising; only last year we realised that the existing boundaries of investigation were not up to the challenges posed by global terrorism and asked parliament for a radical extension of pre-charge detention. Our core criminal justice processes were designed for a different purpose and time. They must continue to evolve to adapt to the very real threat we face.

Monday August 21, 2006
By Craig Murray, London

Ken Jones, president of the Association of Chief Police Officers, appears appalled (Letters, August 19) that I had the temerity to suggest that the police and security services are becoming politicised. Yet in this same letter, he specifically states that the police last year requested longer periods of detention without charge, and he argues that "our core criminal-justice processes ... must continue to evolve to adapt to the very real threat we now face". Mr Jones is a policeman with a deeply political agenda. His "evolution" is a continual increase of police powers and diminution of the rights of the individual. There could be no clearer example than his letter of what it is that makes me uneasy about the politicisation of the police. It used to be their job to enforce the laws, not tell us what they "must" be.

Mr Jones complains that I don't know the facts of the current case. Every "fact" I quoted was sourced by a reputable journalist to the police, security services or Home Office. I just reversed the original spin. I see there is no letter from the Association of Chief Police Officers attacking the hundreds of articles which have hyped the threat and effectively prejudged the accused. If police sources were not so keen to tip the wink to the press on suitcases of bomb-making material, suicide videos and improbable chemistry in plane toilets, then there would have been no need to introduce a note of scepticism.

Sorry, but I can't forget the lies fed to the media about De Menezes, chemical-weapon vests and ricin. Lies fed by the police, up to the highest levels. I am extremely grateful for the work of the police in combating the threat of terrorism regularly since their foundation. I remember with pride those policemen and women who died doing it. Mr Jones's association has much better staff than he deserves. But he must realise that many of us do not agree that Islamic terrorism is historically greater than other threats faced by this country. I do agree there is evil ideology out there, but it comes from Bush and Bin Laden equally.

On 23 August 2016 he persisted:

Eventually we will find out something of the truth behind the alleged terror plot. The law prohibits me from commenting on the evidence: but as the police have already done so, I might say that so far nothing they said has contradicted my contention that no-one had purchased a ticket and nobody had assembled a bomb. It is also worth noting that the mother, Cossor Ali, has not been charged with conspiracy to murder, so the lurid story about her planning to blow up a plane and her baby with a bomb in a feeding bottle appears to be a fantasy.

The charges laid are extremely serious. We will wait to see what the trial brings - unfortunately, the BBC are saying that the prisoners could wait in jail for three years before a substantive trial. As with the "ricin plotters", that is long enough that in the event of a not guilty verdict the public will have forgotten all about it and the media will be able to report it on page 22 in a single paragraph. Who doubts that if the ricin plotters had been found guilty, it would have been page 1 all over again?

Incidentally, my own straw poll indicates that most people don't realise the ricin plot didn't exist and the "plotters" were found not guilty. Hardly surprising when the disgraceful BBC News was today talking about the "Ricin plot" - without mentioning the not guilty verdicts - in a ridiculous scaremongering feature about "Agroterrorism", claiming that terrorists could kill 250,000 people by introducing botulism into a milk tanker. Worth noting that the Head of News and Current Affairs at the BBC is Helen Boaden, whose brother was a New Labour candidate at the last election.

Of course, our still shiny independent Crown Prosecution Service will have impartially assessed the evidence and decided it was sufficient to go to trial - which effectively gave the CPS the power to lock these people up for three years before the evidence is tested by the defence. The CPS mission statement describes itself proudly as "an independent prosecution service".

So, consider the statement by the Crown Prosecution Service at the police conference where the charges were announced on 21 August. I heard this on TV and sat up suddenly. I couldn't believe my ears. I have just tracked down the quote to confirm I heard aright:

Susan Hemmings, Crown Prosecution Service:

"I was briefed in relation to these allegations before the arrest and asked to advise on some preliminary legal issues both before and just after arrest. Together with another senior CPS lawyer, I have been working with the police full time at New Scotland Yard for the last eight days."

What? The CPS unit that took the decision was actually "embedded" with the police investigation in Scotland Yard? Was a party to the turmoil, excitement and indeed hype that has characterised this investigation?

That strikes me as very strange for the body that is meant impartially to assess the weight of police evidence and decide if there is a case for prosecution. Does anyone know if the CPS has ever physically moved itself to Scotland Yard before in any previous case?

Four months later he returned to this case, on 15 December 2006

Google "Rashid Rauf - mastermind". On the first page of

results you will find CBS, the BBC, the Times, Guardian and Mail all describing Rauf last summer, on security service or police briefing, as the "Mastermind" behind the "Liquid terror bomb plot". So the fact that a Pakistani court has found there is no evidence of terrorism against him cannot be lightly dismissed by the cheerleaders of the plot story.

Rashid Rauf still faces other charges, including forgery, and what is touted as possession of explosives, although what he actually possessed was hydrogen peroxide, which is not explosive. As hydrogen peroxide is readily obtainable without limitation from any chemist or hardware store in the UK, why you would source it in Pakistan to blow up jets in Britain was never very convincing. The Pakistani court perhaps felt so too.

Rashid Rauf has much to answer. He is still wanted in the UK over the murder of his uncle some years ago - a crime which, like the alleged forgery, had no apparent terrorist link. None of which adds to the credibility of the evidence he allegedly gave the Pakistani intelligence services about the liquid bomb plot in the UK.

A second and simultaneous development is even more compelling evidence that this massive scare was, as I said at the time, "More propaganda than plot". Thames Valley police have given up after five months scouring the woods near High Wycombe where the bomb materials were allegedly hidden. They told the Home Office on 12 December that they would only continue if the government were prepared to meet the costs; they wished to get back to devoting their resources to real crimes, like armed robbery and burglary.

Remember this was a plot described by the authorities as "Mass murder on an unimaginable scale" and "Bigger than 9/11". There have been instances in the UK of hundreds of police officers deployed for years to find an individual murderer. If the police really believed they were dealing with an effort at "Mass murder on an unimaginable scale", would they be calling off the search after five months? No.

Which brings us to the lies that have been told - one of which concerns this search. An anonymous police source tipped off the media early on that they had discovered a "Suitcase" containing "bomb-making materials". This has recently been described to me by a security service source as "A lot of rubbish from someone's garage dumped in the woods". You could indeed cannibalise bits of old wire, clocks and car parts to form part of a bomb - perhaps you could enclose it in the old suitcase. But have they found stuff that is exclusively concerned with causing explosions, like detonators, explosives or those famous liquid chemicals? No, they haven't found any.

Wycombe Woods, like the sands of Iraq, have failed to yield up the advertised WMD.

The other "evidence" that the police announced they had found consisted of wills (with the implication they were made by suicide bombers) and a map of Afghanistan. It turns out that the wills were made in the early 90s by volunteers going off to fight the Serbs in Bosnia - they had been left with the now deceased uncle of one of those arrested. The map of Afghanistan had been copied out by an eleven year old boy. All of which is well known to the UK media, but none of which has been reported for fear of prejudicing the trial. I am at a complete loss to understand why it does not prejudice the trial for police to announce in a blaze of worldwide front page publicity that they have found bomb-making materials, wills and maps. Only if you contradict the police is that prejudicial. Can anyone explain why?

While the arrest of 26 people in connection with the plot was also massively publicised, the gradual release of many of them has again gone virtually unreported. For example on 31 October a judge released two brothers from Chingford commenting that the police had produced no credible evidence against them. Charges against others have been downgraded, so that those now accused of plotting to commit explosions are less than the ten planes the police claimed they planned to blow up in suicide attacks.

Five British newspapers had to pay damages to a Birmingham man they accused, on security service briefing, of being part of the plot. Only the Guardian had the grace to publish the fact and print a retraction.

A final fact to ponder. Despite naming him as the "mastermind" behind something "bigger than 9/11", the British government made no attempt to extradite Rashid Rauf on charges of terrorism. That is not difficult to do - the Pakistani authorities have handed over scores of terrorist suspects to the US, many into the extraordinary rendition process, and on average the procedure is astonishingly quick - less than a week and they are out of the country. But the British security services, who placed so much weight on intelligence from Rashid Rauf, were extraordinarily coy about getting him here where his evidence could be properly scrutinised by a British court. However MI5 were greatly embarrassed by Birmingham police, who insisted on pointing out that Rauf was wanted in the UK over the alleged murder of his uncle in Birmingham. Now he was in custody in Pakistan, shouldn't we extradite him? So eventually an extradition request over that murder was formally submitted - but not pursued with real energy or effort. There remains no sign that we will see Rauf in the UK.

I still do not rule out that there was a germ of a terror plot at the heart of this investigation. We can speculate about agents provocateurs and security service penetration, both British and Pakistani, but still there might have been genuine terrorists involved. But the incredible disruption to the traveling public, the War on Shampoo, and the "Bigger than 9/11" hype is unraveling You won't read that in the newspapers.

Secret Confessions and Torture

Mohammed Sheikh Khalid has now, voluntarily and of his own free will, admitted he masterminded every significant event from the Norman Invasion through the bubonic plague, fall of Constantinople, and Great Fire of London, to the Battle of Little Big Horn, assassination of JFK and the Oklahoma bombing.

Or he might as well have. The extraordinarily comprehensive list of terrorist outrages for which he claims responsibility would be beyond the capacity of any but the most brilliant and inspired mortal; Khalid, I fear, is a more run of the mill thug.

But in truth, we have absolutely no idea what, if anything, he has confessed at all. The BBC brazenly reported all of yesterday that while Khalid did allege he had been tortured during his four years of secret detention by the CIA in various locations around the globe, he is now freely confessing under no duress and does not retract any of his confession.

Who says? The proceedings being held in Guantanamo Bay, and which the BBC report so uncritically, are held behind barbed wire, machine guns, gun emplacements, reinforced steel and concrete and combination locks, before an exclusively military panel. Khalid does not even have a lawyer present. For all we know, his confession could be an entire fabrication. The blandness of the BBC reporting in these circumstances is one of the worst examples of the appalling desertion of the principles of that once worthwhile institution.

The readiness of the rest of the media to push the "instill fear" button on behalf of the Orwellian government is predictable. They report as fact that Khalid also planned to blow up Heathrow, Canary Wharf, Big Ben, Buckingham Palace and any other British building the

Pentagon had heard of.

If Khalid really is freely and openly confessing all of this stuff, then what possible reason can there be to deny him a lawyer, and not allow public and media access to his trial? The atrocities he allegedly confesses - the Twin Towers, Madrid, Bali - left thousands of bereaved families. They have a right to see justice done, rather than this elaborate propaganda set-up, with its total lack of proper legal process or intellectual credibility.

Did Khalid really do all of this? Two facts must be considered. He has been through years of vicious torture and of solitary confinement. If the experience of others who survived extraordinary rendition is typical, he has been kept in total isolation, in darkness, beaten, cut, suffocated and drowned, suffered white noise and sensory deprivation. He will have been moved around, often not even knowing which country he is in. One good contact has told me that the CIA gave the Uzbek torturers their turn with him. I do not know that for certain, but who can contradict me?

After years of this, a person can be so psychologically damaged that they believe the narrative of their torturers to be the truth. It is perfectly possible that he now in fact believes he did all that stuff on the list, when he did not.

Alternatively, he may have decided to exaggerate his own role and achievements for the personal glory it brings. We can get the appalling situation where both the sides which benefit from and wish to promote the War on Terror - Al Qaida and the CIA - indulge in what becomes a grim mutual cooperation in exaggeration as each seeks to glorify their role. Thus do those on both sides who actually desire a "Clash of Civilisations", promote one.

What is happening now in Guantanamo Bay is a disgrace. We cannot in present circumstances accept anything that comes out of it as other than a completely unsubstantiated claim by the Pentagon. Some of it is quite possibly true. But this is no way to make the case.

The Right To Offend

The "War on Terror" had led to a climate of Islamophobia in the UK, and Muslim communities were impacted by heavy policing and suspension of civil rights under anti-terror legislation. In this atmosphere of tension, Muslim anger erupted over the publication in Denmark of cartoons depicting the Prophet Mohammed.

Demonstration by Muslims across Europe, including in the UK, in which there were calls for the death of the cartoonist, further stoked Islamophobia in a vicious circle. As somebody who had been campaigning very prominently in defence of the Islamic community, Craig Murray felt the need to define his opinion.

This article was published on 6 February 2006.

Having spent so much time expressing concern over issues which impact, not only but primarily, on Muslims, both in Uzbekistan and the West, I should like to give a few thoughts about the recent controversy over cartoons of the Prophet Mohammed.

First, I will start by saying that I am myself a monotheist. I believe in God, and have never understood why the three great monotheistic religions spend their time arguing over detail. I was brought up myself in a Christian tradition, and I believe that it taught me many excellent ethical values and gave useful insights into life. I believe that the majority of Jews and Muslims gain equally valid insights from teachings that are more similar than is generally commented upon. I have never given much value to the more magical, or as the Church would say mysterious, elements in the story telling of the faith. They are metaphors. Many of them are shared with Judaism and Islam, and each has some uniquely its own.

I have also felt personally most comfortable with those who emphasise a close personal relationship with God, be they Quakers or Methodists, or from the Sufi tradition in Uzbekistan. I believe that faith should be respected, and that you should not lightly belittle somebody's faith or belief.

But faith is a personal thing, and if someone finds your belief laughable or threatening, they should be completely entitled to express that. I would not myself draw a cartoon of the Prophet Mohammed, or write the last scene of 'Jerry Springer the Opera', because I would not like to cause unnecessary offence. But I would not in any way prevent others from doing so if they want.

Muslims have every right to believe that nobody should caricature Mohammed, and presumably Muslims don't do such things. However they have no right to stop anyone else from producing cartoons, commenting on the age of Mohammed's wives (whatever his relationship with them), or saying whatever else they wish on the subject. You cannot enforce the strictures of your faith on non-believers. The World is not a religiously ordered society. That may come when you die, or not, we'll find out soon enough.

Religions need to be caricatured. God and faith may be perfect, but men are not, and throughout history religious structures have been used to exert social control, give power to a hierarchy, and to make money from the gullible. Religion has always been distorted to justify both war and repression of people's rights, and still is today, by Osama Bin Laden, George W Bush, and others. The dangers of protecting religion from ridicule are obvious.

So I don't agree with the protesters who have sparked such concern, and I think they are very foolish indeed to appear to be threatening violence. In general, it is dangerous to prosecute people for what they write or say, but there does seem to me a case that some may have had an intent to incite violence, which can be dealt with without any new illiberal anti-terrorist laws. But a real sense of proportion is needed here, and we have to aim off for those used to a political culture where extreme language is more acceptable but not literally meant. It seems to me the use of police cautions might be sensible at this stage.

It is particularly important that this is not used to build up steam behind Tony Blair's ridiculous proposal to ban Hizb-ut-Tehrir. That organisation remains key in that it has the most fundamentalist Islamic views, many of which I personally dislike, but actively preach non-violence at that end of the religious spectrum.

Unfortunately, voices of tolerance on all sides are going to be in short supply in the mainstream punditry in the next few days. Religion still can be manipulated to bring out the worst in people, but we should not forget that it operates more effectively in doing precisely the opposite.

The Sentencing of Saddam Hussein
5 November 2006.

I hold no brief for Saddam Hussein. He is a gruesome dictator who is much better out of power, and a dangerous man who is much better in captivity. I am nonetheless sorry he will be murdered by the State. Iraq has seen quite enough death already, and like so many of the others, this will merely engender more. Hundreds of thousands of Iraqis have died already due to the Bush/Blair invasion. The vast majority of them were totally innocent. If you kill hundreds of thousands of innocent people, you are bound to kill the odd guilty one from time to time, whether by accident or design. That is the measure of the Bush/Blair achievement.

This death, just like that of al-Zaqarwi, will be hailed as a "Turning-point" by the invaders, their leaders, puppets and media spokesmen. So was the capture of Saddam, so were the elections, so was the formation of the government, so was the disbanding of the army. It is unsurprising that there have been so many - a downward spiral is just an unending circle of turning points, and Iraq has been embarked on a helter-skelter ride to Hell. Given what came after him, Bush/Blair have achieved the near impossible feat of making Saddam Hussein look like a comparatively better leader for the Iraqi people.

The trial itself was a political charade with the Americans as puppeteers. Judges were repeatedly changed if they showed any sign of independent thought. Defence lawyers who looked too effective were simply murdered. The TV cameras were turned off on the show trial if it got sticky for the US - with an American hand on the button. And the ultimate in stage management, the verdict was handed down two days before the US mid-term elections. Who honestly does not believe that timing was contrived?

I am all in favour of Dictators and War Criminals being punished. I wish Saddam had received a fair trial, and think the Hague would have been much better - he would have been seen to get a fair trial, and I am pretty sure a fair guilty verdict. We should not lose sight of the need to hold justice over the mighty. Bush and Blair are responsible for the unprovoked invasion of a sovereign state, against the wishes of the UN Security Council. They have on their hands the blood of hundreds of thousands of people. I live and hope that I will see the day when they are in the dock.

I will still be against the death penalty.

Speech to the Conference Against Islamophobia
London 19 November 2006

As many of you know, I stood against Jack Straw in Blackburn at the last election. People in that constituency have been wearing the niqab for many, many ears, certainly for all the time he's been MP. Why now, suddenly, for the first time, did it start to worry him? It was a considered, calculated move, in a column written quietly in private and submitted to the newspaper, and an effort to jump onto the bandwagon of Islamophobia, that was so quickly followed up by other cabinet members that there can be no doubt that it was planned beforehand.

This fear of a strip of cloth is not entirely new in the UK. I was actually going to come and speak to you in my kilt today. I didn't do it because we are a bit near the fire limit and I was a bit worried about the possible effects of an outbreak of uncontrolled lust.

However, 250 years ago, not that long ago, the wearing of the kilt was punishable by death. Then it got not quite so draconian and it was only punishable by transportation, which is why there are so many Craigs in Australia. But that kind of ridiculous attitude to costume is not one which I thought we would see a government in this country attempting to bring back.

I am not a Muslim myself. I am not particularly religious myself. I believe that Islam, like many other religions, contains a great deal of good in its ethical teachings. I also believe that Islam, like other religions, is capable of being perverted by leadership structures for evil as well as for good.

I am not here to defend Islam in particular. I am here to defend everybody's right to pursue their own religion, and that is what everybody in this hall believes in.

When I was in Uzbekistan I saw many people tortured for their religion, tortured with terrible tortures including boiling alive, including mutilation of the genitals, and drowning. And the West was receiving intelligence from Uzbekistan, via the CIA, as a result of that torture. And it's worth noting, when Tony Blair talks, and the Americans talk, that perhaps we'll open a dialogue with Iran and Syria, at the same time they have been talking about Syria on the surface as the axis of evil, at the same time they have been sending Muslims to Syria to be tortured as part of the extraordinary rendition programme. That's how genuine their motives are.

As a result of this torture I saw in Uzbekistan, I challenged within the system intelligence which was simply untrue, which enormously exaggerated the strength of Al Qaida, which named individuals as members of Al Qaida who plainly were not, not just in Uzbekistan, but throughout the World.

I queried this, I questioned it, I was summoned back to meetings in London where I said we are getting intelligence which is not true. I was told it was operationally useful. Nobody ever argued with me when I said it was untrue, but they said it was operationally useful because that is how intelligence is judged nowadays. The intelligence on Iraqi Weapons of Mass Destruction was untrue, but it was operationally useful if your purpose was to start an illegal war; and false intelligence which vastly exaggerates the strength of Al Qaida, and which exaggerates the so-called Islamic extremist threat to the UK, is operationally useful to them now, because they can use it to blacked Muslims, and to stir up Islamophobia in the UK.

And that is what we are now seeing. And when Eliza Manningham Buller claims there are 1600 active terrorists, not sympathisers, active Muslim terrorists, in the UK, she is not exaggerating, she is not hyping, she is lying, and deliberately lying.

That's quite enough of Eliza Mainwaring-Hitler or whatever her name is.

You know, we are seeing such a tide of Islamophobia, stoked by government ministers, not just by individuals, so that anything a Muslim does is front page news, no matter how small, no matter if it's a matter of planning permission for a prayer room in Windsor – that's worse than a murder by a non-Muslim.

How have we got to this stage? We have got to this stage because the government has deliberately stoked it; has stoked it to create a climate of fear, so that when we hear of the deaths of 650,000 people in Iraq, or 100,000 people in Afghanistan, or people to come in Iran or elsewhere, they hope that we will see Muslims as dehumanised, and they won't get the public protest, because ordinary people will think: "Well, they were only Muslims, and they are trying to kill us too."

We are not going to fall for this trick. The British people have not accepted it, and we will not accept it.

I was not afraid to tell the government hard truths. I have not been afraid to continue to tell hard truths since I left, and I am not afraid to tell some hard truths which are uncomfortable for us in the anti-war movement as well.

One of these truths is that sadly the Muslim community is unaware, is sleepwalking towards disaster and is still maintaining a pathetic loyalty to the Labour Party which is persecuting it.

When I stood against Jack Straw in Blackburn I was not allowed to enter any mosque in the constituency due to a decision by the Lancashire Council of Mosques. Yvonne Ridley had similar problems in Leicester. That has not massively changed. Without huge effort on our part to explain what is happening, to get it over, to get through patriarchal systems, to get through tribal and other loyalties, to involve people in democratic politics in a reasoned way, not a Tammany Hall way, without that effort, we are not going to make progress.

We have to be out there. I see many people at meeting in London. I see many intellectuals from the Muslim community expressing themselves with me on university platforms and in newspaper columns.

Where I need to see people is out there with me when I am speaking and campaigning and knocking on doors in Bolton and Bradford and Blackburn because that is where this will be won, on the streets. On the streets.

I was a member of the Anti Nazi League back in the 70s and 80s, in the days when Peter Hain and Phil Woolas were on our side of the barricades, not on the side with the racists. I know it can be done. I know Islamophobia can be beaten back, but it's a long, hard and unglamorous grind, and we need all of us there, in there fighting together.

Thank you.

Dundee University

Craig Murray put his name forward for election as Rector of his alma mater, a longstanding ambition of his. This interview appeared in the Dundee Courier on 2nd February 2007.

One of the leading candidates to become Dundee University rector has heavily criticised proposed cuts to the institution's staff and courses to claw back a '1.6 million deficit.

Craig Murray, former British ambassador to Uzbekistan, has spoken out against the plant that could see town planning and modern languages courses axed - along with up to 100 staff. Mr Murray echoed concerns raised by the UCU that an artificial financial crisis had been created by a campus development programme that has seen millions spent on new buildings.

"I am very worried about the university's desire to cut staff and cut the languages department," he said. "I'm not at all sure the financial situation justifies it.

"I have been studying the figures and we do not need job loses, and certainly not in courses where the university interacts with the community such as with modern languages."

When announcing plans for cut-backs the university suggested there would be "significant cost reductions and efficiency improvements" affecting the library, the estates service and research and innovation services. The university is also planning to increase income from sources such as overseas students and postgraduate students to try to turn a 1% budget deficit ('1.6 million) into a 3% surplus by 2010 to 2011. That will require a change in the difference between spending and income totaling '6.85 million

Mr Murray suggested excessive amounts of money had

been spent on unneeded layers of bureaucracy and administration rather than university teaching resources. He said he also believed the large outlays on recent building programmes undertaken by the university distorted its financial situation and were being used as an excuse to enforce changes.

"It seems there is no need for these cuts, and I believe the reason they are being pursued is part of an agenda rather than financial prudence.

"Only the smallest restructuring of the university's debt would make the savings required to meet the targets set".

Staff, students and the UCU have already vented their anger. Many are worried the changes could affect the university's links with the local community as well as hampering its ability to attract students. Staff and students are planning to fight the proposed cuts ahead of the February 19 university court meeting, which will decide on the way ahead.

However, university management have insisted the capital investment in buildings and equipment over the past four years has been fully justified. It also highlighted the fact research income was high but was not growing as quickly as it had, and its financial status was not sustainable for the long or medium term.

This interview with John Crace appeared in the Guardian Education on 13 February 2007

A one-bedroomed flat in Shepherd's Bush isn't many people's idea of a former diplomat's des res. And it probably isn't Craig Murray's, either. But after a bruising few years, which have seen him forced out of his job as ambassador to Uzbekistan by the Foreign and Commonwealth Office (FCO) for failing to toe the British line on intelligence obtained under torture, come close to bankruptcy, when he started a legal challenge against his dismissal, and navigate his way through a tricky divorce, he's happy to settle for what he can get.

You wouldn't blame him for seeking out a quiet life - and by contesting this Friday's election for the post of rector of Dundee University against a former Scottish rugby international, Andy Nicoll, it might look as if Murray had already got his slippers half on. After all, what could be more suitable for an ex His Excellency than an honorary position that requires little more than dressing up in fancy clothes from time to time, eating the odd formal banquet and smoking an after-dinner Havana? If Lorraine Kelly has been able to handle the job for the past two and a half years or so, then it should be a doddle for Murray.

Looking after students' interests

This isn't quite the way Murray sees it, though. "Being rector may be unpaid, but it should be more than a glorified PR non-job," he says. "I was head of the student union when I was at Dundee in the early 1980s, so I know what a rector is meant to do. The post was originally established so that students had an elected representative to look after their interests in the running of the university; this function has rather been neglected in recent years as the administration has been left to the principal. But I intend to be much more hands-on."

In other words, he's planning to do exactly what he did at the Foreign Office: ask difficult questions and be bloody-minded. Murray gives a half-smile. "If necessary," he says cautiously. So take that as a yes. Dundee University is going through tough times; it's running a '1.8m deficit and the principal, Sir Alan Langmeads, has put forward a cost-cutting plan that includes up to 100 redundancies, the closure of the modern languages department and shorter opening hours for the library.

Murray doesn't much care for it and neither, he reckons, do many others. "I can't really see how introducing new layers of bureaucracy and cutting academic provision is in the university's best interests," he says, "and I believe that many students feel too powerless to influence policy and that academics are scared about speaking up because they are worried about losing their jobs. If I could be a rallying point - the rector is the third most powerful university post - then maybe we could have a proper democratic debate about the best way forward."

With no full-time job at present - he doesn't count writing a book as a proper career - Murray describes his occupation as "dissident". Not that he looks much like your archetypal dissident. He's a little tired and distant around the eyes, but that's the only outward sign of a life in conflict. Even so, dissident is not as wide of the mark as you might think.

Murray grew up in Norfolk, where his father was stationed at an RAF base, and his childhood appears to have been the usual unremarkable mix of home and school.

Except Murray hated his school with a passion. "The Paston was an old-fashioned grammar that was trying its best to be an independent school," he says. "It felt as if the teachers were still fighting the second world war, and once a week we were all made to dress up in military uniform and become cadets. Either I skipped school or refused to take part, so I was frequently suspended. Anyway, the overall result was that I did little work and managed to screw up my A-levels spectacularly."

Things improved when he went up to Dundee - "it was the only university that would have me; I got in through clearing" - but though he emerged four academic years and two student officer sabbatical years later with a first in history, he still couldn't find a job.

"You'd have thought that a decent degree and time spent as head of the student union might have been of interest to someone," he laughs, "but I must have applied for more than 100 jobs and only one firm even wrote back to me. It was the early 80s, there were about three and half million people unemployed and I was a bit desperate, so I took the fast-stream civil service exam as a bit of a joke."

Things became less funny when Murray not only passed the exam but sailed through the two-day selection panel. "I then had to work out what I wanted to do," he says. "I'd never had any great desire to travel or see the world - I only discovered what a pizza was during a trip to see a girl-friend in Chicago when I was 21 - and I only put down the diplomatic corps because it seemed marginally more glamorous than anything else on offer. I couldn't face the idea of joining the Department of Health and Social Security or the Inland Revenue; it would have been like admitting I was really dull and had no friends."

Murray was a bit of an outsider from the start in the Foreign Office. "It likes to boast about how it has broadened access," he says, "but it's a complete nonsense. When the FCO talks about graduate entry it actually means to all levels of the service, and you virtually need a degree even to empty a wastepaper basket there these days. Of the 22 people in my high-flier intake, only two of us didn't go to Oxbridge and only I didn't go to a public school."

Even so, he proved himself to be a safe enough pair of hands and, after successful junior postings in Poland, Nigeria and Ghana, he was offered the top job as ambassador to Uzbekistan in 2002 when he was in his early 40s. Post 9/11, the former Russian republic wasn't the diplomatic backwater it once had been and most FCO insiders reckoned Murray was headed for the top: a safe tour of Uzbekistan and a stint as a European ambassador, before bowing out with one of the plum jobs and a knighthood, was the general forecast.

It all started to unravel within weeks of his arriving in Tashkent. "President Karimov was making a big deal of a forthcoming terrorist trial," Murray says, "so I thought I would go along to watch. It was all going to script with the accused admitting that his nephews belonged to al-Qaida, when the man burst into tears, saying it was all untrue and that he'd been tortured into a confession. I was close enough to touch him in court and I could tell he was speaking the truth."

Murray didn't need to go digging for more evidence: as he had shown an interest in these abuses by turning up in court, dissidents from all parts of the country came to the embassy to tell their stories. To his amazement, he soon realised there was a distinct overlap between the confessions that had been extracted under torture and the security intelligence that was being circulated by the CIA.

No hero
"You have to realise I never set out to be a hero," he insists. "I was never a great campaigner for human rights. In many ways, I'd always been just as compromised as any other diplomat. When I was working on the South African desk of the London office I had had to send out letters saying we believed that the African National Congress was a terrorist organisation. I didn't think that for a second and nor did anyone else I was working with, but we did it because it was the price of an impartial, depoliticised civil service.

"The closest I had ever got to any form of stand was by refusing to implement a government directive to persuade the Poles to reduce the size of the health warnings on cigarette packets to conform with EU law.

But the situation in Uzbekistan was very different. This was about torture and it seemed very black and white to me. It still does; the only surprise was that it didn't seem to be a moral issue for other members of the government and the FCO."

Within a few months, Murray was getting a telegram from the FCO suggesting he was "focusing too much on human rights issues" and, when this had no effect, he was told outright that Britain was entitled to use intelligence obtained under torture providing it wasn't the Brits who were doing the torturing. "It was legal, it was policy and I was to shut up," he says.

But he didn't, and in August 2003 he was recalled to London from a family holiday in Canada. "I was told that if I resigned from Uzbekistan I would be given the embassy in Copenhagen," he continues. "It would have been a huge promotion, but I refused on principle. I was then told that I had a week to resign or I would face 18 charges, including being an alcoholic, selling British visas for sexual favours and stealing from the embassy.

"All the charges were fabricated, but there was nothing I could do to defend myself, as I was also told I wasn't allowed to discuss the charges with anyone or call anybody as a witness. The FCO would conduct its own investigation and let me know the outcome - which was never going to be in doubt."

Murray returned to Tashkent, but within days was flown back to the psychiatric ward of St Thomas's Hospital in London. "I was in a complete state of collapse," he says. "I could barely speak or move and I doubted anyone would believe my story. Fortunately the psychiatrist said to me, 'You don't need me, you need a good lawyer' and proceeded to get in contact with Gareth Peirce [the human rights lawyer who defended the Birmingham Six]."

From that point on, things began to look up for Murray.

He was cleared of all the allegations, except, bizarrely, for the one of discussing the others with another person - "technically, they were right as I did discuss it with my secretary, but as they were found to be false..." - and he was given a substantial financial settlement in return.

But he did still lose his job. Which is how Murray really comes to be in Dundee this week. And what if the students vote for Nicoll instead? "I'll be disappointed," he says, "but at least there's not a salary riding on it." So how is he managing for money? "The book didn't sell as well in hardback as I had hoped, but I've done well out of the film rights. They were initially bought by Michael Winterbottom - and he's still making the movie - but he's flogged the rights on to Paramount."

His role will be played by Steve Coogan. Is he worried about being turned into a joke? "No. Winterbottom's got a good track record and, besides, some of the story is quite amusing anyway." Nice to know someone can still see the funny side.

INSTALLATION SPEECH AS RECTOR OF THE UNIVERSITY OF DUNDEE

ADDRESS GIVEN UPON THE OCCASION OF HIS
INSTALLATION
AS RECTOR OF THE UNIVERSITY OF DUNDEE
By
CRAIG J MURRAY Esq, MA(Hons)
In the
BONAR HALL, DUNDEE
26 September 2007
Under the Title of:
WHY LONDON SHOULD STOP WORRYING ABOUT
SCOTTISH INDEPENDENCE – WE CAN STILL RULE
ENGLAND FROM BRUSSELS

Vice-Chancellor, My Dear Friends,

It is most kind of you to come along here today as I receive the singular honour of being made Rector of my own University.

I arrive here following our tradition of an idiosyncratic pub crawl known as the Rectorial Drag. That sounds like an occasion for which I should be picking out a nice skirt and blouse – which as some of my former student colleagues here will tell you would not be the first time. The Rectorial Drag however is an occasion where the students pull their new Rector through the streets in a carriage, from City Hall to University, entering the pubs on the way. I can honestly say it is the first time I have ever been dragged to a pub. Dragged out, yes. Chucked out, frequently. Dragged in is a new one.

By chance it is thirty years almost to the day since I arrived, bewildered, into freshers' week, clutching everything I owned in one cardboard box and a battered

BOAC flight bag.

Little did I dream that thirty years later I would become Rector of the place. Certainly not – I expected to be much too busy being Prime Minister.

In that distant first week I attended the Rectorial Installation of Sir Clement Freud. He was a man of great wit and perspicacity, and his installation address was hilarious. Sadly, as we all know, decline and decay is the natural order of things, and with the passing years Sir Clement declined to the extent that he eventually became Rector of St Andrews.

These occasions traditionally involve a certain amount of knockabout humour, and I am sure that no offence will be taken. We look in fact with fond regard to our sister institution south of the Tay Estuary, marking with sadness the scent of her senile decline, as we might an elderly relative whom we care about but are grateful we don't have to live with.

I believe that Clement Freud was the only one of my predecessors to have made that particular error. Stephen Fry was invited to stand at St Andrews but sensibly declined. They can always try again when he's 70.

All of which brings me to note what a tremendously talented bunch my predecessors as Rector have been. Here I give the obligatory tip of the hat to Sir Peter Ustinov.

I am biased in the case of two of them, George Mackie and Gordon Wilson, because I was the seconder of one and proposer of the other. That made my own election my third successful rectorial campaign, and I claim the record, to be beaten when I am re-elected in 2010.

Getting elected is of course the difficult bit. My own election was fiercely contested and the result was close. I would like to pay a sincere tribute to Andy Nicol, a real gentleman, for his well-fought and constructive campaign, and for being such a good loser. Though, of course, as a former captain of the British Lions rugby team he did have a great deal of practice.

One excellent piece of electioneering by my opponent was securing the entire front page of the election day Dundee edition of the Daily Record. Most of the page was taken up by a picture of Andy and the headline screamed "I was born to lead Dundee Students". The Daily Record is a paper which is at least consistent in its standard of accuracy.

The flaw in this great ploy, achieved with considerable effort, was of course that not many of our electorate are Daily Record readers. Some folk surmised that this mistake came about because Scottish Labour HQ were under the impression the election was at the University of Abertay.

Anyway, it was a good bit of electioneering, and made even better by the fact that in this special edition of the Daily Record, my two immediate predecessors, not without some encouragement from within the University hierarchy, chose to endorse the candidature of my opponent.

The Record told us "Outgoing Rector Lorraine Kelly and comedian Fred Macaulay threw their weight behind Nicol as the former Scotland captain urged the University's Record readers to vote for him in the polls today."

I believe the University's Record readers both did.

I don't regard former Rectors campaigning for a candidate – and thus perforce campaigning against a candidate – as quite the done thing. But it is still potentially effective electioneering. The only downside I see is that, should the ploy fail and someone else get elected, and were that person in the least bit vindictive, that person would then have a great platform in front of the entire University to get his own back. I do see that potential danger, don't you?

Some of you will be relieved, and some disappointed, to hear that I do not intend to do this. I am very glad that my predecessor, Lorraine Kelly, was Rector of this University. Otherwise she might have gone her entire life without ever seeing the inside of an institute of higher education.

The other ex-Rector involved was Fred Macaulay, apparently a local comedian, though that is not obvious from reading his rectorial address. In the most striking passage, Fred tells us he does a great impression of Sean Connery, adding "Hey, I'm bald and Scottish, how hard can it be?"

Very hard, Fred, very hard. Sean Connery is bald, Scottish and immensely talented. Fred, however, is more like this egg: bald, Scottish and easily crushed. (Breaks egg).

I did say we should have some knockabout stuff, and seriously Fred was a hard-working and popular Rector. I am sure he'll come up with some much better jokes about me.

Now this is going to be a very dull afternoon if I just ramble on like this and you just gawp at me. We need some atmospherics – feel free to laugh and cheer, or clap or shout "Rubbish" when you want to. Above all do heckle. Heckling is a fine tradition. The very word comes from Dundee.

Heckling is a process in the jute industry. To heckle is to comb out the jute prior to spinning. It was a tough, manual job and the heckling shops were murky with dust that choked the lungs. The hecklers were famous for their radicalism, probably a reaction to their terrible working conditions, and would turn up and yell at politicians. I think that's quite right – present company accepted I don't recall ever meeting a politician who did not ought to be shouted at. Thus the hecklers yelled, and the verb "To heckle" jumped from a textile process to a political barracking. Uniquely, as far as I know, what other student unions call election hustings, DUSA called election hecklings.

One appalling development in modern politics is the death of heckling.

Nowadays politicians deliver their sound-bites to a pathetically complacent and complicit media, in front of a carefully selected and vetted audience of the faithful. Just try getting close enough to a politician to heckle them. I mean that literally – please do try. When someone does manage, like Walter Wolfgang, the eighty year old who shouted "Rubbish" at Jack Straw, they are likely to be manhandled and arrested under the laughably named Prevention of Terrorism Act.

Jack Straw, incidentally, is a man who should have "Rubbish" shouted at him from the moment he steps out of the shower in the morning until the moment he retires with his evening cocoa.

The peculiar criminalisation of heckling is part of the most extraordinary onslaught on our civil liberties. Here in Dundee a woman was arrested under the Prevention of Terrorism Act for walking on a cycle path. That is true – Google it. And last year we had the extraordinary incident of the Special Branch walking around Fresher's Fayre. That is something which I promise you will not happen again. A university is no place for the thought police. We have no terrorists here; what our students are thinking is our students' business. That is why they are here: to think.

The Rectorial Address is a great tradition, and I am standing here on the shoulders of giants. Those who have delivered their rectorial address at Scottish universities include figures like William Gladstone, Adam Smith, Andrew Carnegie and JM Barrie. These addresses were great occasions. They have their traditions and their protocols. They have on occasion been highly rumbustuous, and sometimes speeches have been fiery and partisan.

I have however been told that the recent style has been for speeches to be non-political and uncontroversial. So I gave a great deal of thought to a suitably bland title for this address, and I came up with:

"Why London Should Stop Worrying about Scottish Independence Because We Scots Can Still Rule England From Brussels."

Nothing to argue with there, I think.

The truth is, my whole life I have believed that there is no point in getting on your back legs and opening your mouth in public, unless you are really going to say something. It may not sound very radical, but the vast majority of speakers, particularly in modern politics, manage to sound off for ages without actually saying anything at all. Our Prime Minister – another former Scottish University Rector – did so in his big conference speech last week. That certainly ought not to happen inside universities, but I am afraid it does.

A university must be a place of stimulating intellectual debate across not only the myriad topics of academia, but on the issues of the day affecting society as a whole. The best minds must clash and spark, and students must be fully and intellectually engaged. A university must constitute a vast whirring machinery of the mind, reacting to and operating on the wider society of which it forms an integral part. It must be a place of the liveliest and best informed debate, where no subject is out of bounds, or over-respected, or immune from the heat of debate. A university must be a democratic discussion. If it is not that, it is not a university.

We must be unapologetic that a University is about much, much more than training to get a job. The over-emphasis of vocational training bedevils higher education. Of course your career is important; but you have the entire rest of your life to be a slave to it. You don't have to start now. The student who concentrates purely on his future career leaves here equipped for only a small part of life. I learnt vastly more in discussions with people of other academic, social, cultural and ethnic backgrounds in bars and kitchens, and from private reading, than I ever did in the lecture theatre. In my formal university learning I acquired skills of logic, analysis, ordering and debate. A University Education must teach you to think, not just to stack widgets. And that is true across every one of our disciplines – as relevant to nurses and dentists as to lawyers.

Scotland has a great intellectual tradition based on this radical liberal concept. Scotland had a prototype of universal education two centuries before England, and had five universities for centuries when England only had two.

I would like now to quote from an essay by Lindsay Paterson, Professor of Educational Policy at the University of Edinburgh, published in 2020, Agenda for a New Scotland, Luath Press 2005. I am going to break a golden rule of speechmaking and read at length from Professor Paterson, because this states what I believe more eloquently than I can express it, and I believe this is a vastly important essay which everyone involved in Scottish universities should read. Professor Paterson's aim is to sketch out the principles on which Scottish education should be based:

The first premise is to insist on the emancipatory potential of intellectual, serious, theoretical and difficult learning. If secondary schools and universities are not about that, then they are barely worth having. "Relevance" is something we learn with experience, and experience can only be experienced, not taught; we cannot judge relevance unless we have already grasped the principles of a system of understanding. In particular, therefore, vocational courses are not what initial education should be about. They are about training for specific jobs. Where they are not best done on the job itself, learning from the accumulated wisdom of more experienced colleagues (whatever the line of work), they presuppose a body of theoretical knowledge and understanding that ought to be engaged with first. Practice without theory is blind.

... Second, since the building of an efficient economic system ought never to be an end in itself, but only the means to such goals as building a fair, democratic and culturally enriching society, an equally important premise has to be that programmes of general liberal education are better at preparing people for life as decent citizens than any other kind of learning. That was something which the old radicals understood well. You could make citizens for the new era of mass democracy by equipping them with the cultural capacities which the aristocratic or bourgeois ruling class had acquired through their education. Citizenship was not something to be segregated into discrete programmes, but should permeate many types of study – literature, history, geography, politics, science, religion. The student who learns how to debate the meaning of a poem by Liz Lochead, or a novel by Alisdair Gray, or a film by Paul Lavery, or to weigh the evidence for and against wind farms or genetic modification, or to understand the reasons why Islam and Christianity have sometimes been in conflict is in fact well prepared for life as a citizen of Scotland.

Third, we need therefore a debate about cultural purposes. This is where new radical thinking is urgently needed. Although I have been arguing that we should recover the old idea that democratising access to a general, liberal education is the only programme that is truly radical, it would not be radical simply to adopt uncritically the content of pedagogical methods that would have constituted such a programme in earlier eras. For example, the culture to which students should now be exposed is certainly not the unitary one of even half a century ago. In Scotland, we inherit ideas from Islam as well as from Christianity, literature by women as well as by men, working class political ideas as well as middle class ones, Scottish philosophical thought as well as Anglo-Saxon. We have to make selections from a potentially enormous set of curricular options. The guiding principles might be partly the intellectual capacities that we want to be the outcome for students. But it can't be only that ... there have to be moral, aesthetic and other judgements about the value of particular knowledge, unfashionable though that is at a time when values are supposed to be inherently relative and the curriculum is supposed to be only about developing competences ...

What should we reasonably expect our graduates to know and be able to do, at an advanced level? Is it sufficient to say that their broad cultural and intellectual preparation has finished at school, or should we expect something more? At the moment, to be frank, we don't even know whether and to what extent existing programmes of higher education are any kind of common basis for citizenship at all.

I am entirely with Professor Paterson, but it is fair to say that almost all the contributions I have heard from others within the governing bodies of the University have been tending to the opposite, with an increasingly narrow vocational focus. The need for students to get a job on leaving has always been there. The lack of grants and the tuition fees paid by some of our students add to the pressures. But my generation graduated into a labour market with three and a half million unemployed and few opportunities. But the idea that our university experience should be solely about finding a job would rightly have been laughed out of court. People are marvellous things, so much more than simply machines for economic production. Indeed, I would say that is the aspect of them that has the least to do with a university.

Professor Paterson sets his thoughts within a specifically Scottish tradition. That is appropriate today – we are a university open to the world and with a worldwide reputation, but we are also Scottish, as testifies the fact that I stand before you today in the uniquely Scottish position of Rector, elected by the students.

Becoming Rector here fulfils two of my great ambitions in life. The first was when I had a Highland Reel named after me, written by in my view Scotland's best traditional music exponents the Battlefield Band. Sadly the great Jimmy Shand is no longer with us, but I like to imagine it at ceilidhs – "Our next set is a highland reel, with The Lang Heid followed by Lady Margaret Campbell of Glenlyon followed by Ambassador Craig Murray of Tashkent." That will confuse them.

So my very own reel a great honour, and my first ambition. My second was to become Rector of the University of Dundee.

I might have to give up on the third, as I don't suppose Kylie Minogue would be up for it.

You will have noted that my robe is rather plainer than many of the gorgeous ones around. That may surprise you in such an elevated office. The Rector is the second most senior officer of the University. In the University's foundation document, the Charter, Article 4 says "There shall be a Chancellor of the University who shall be the head of the University". Article 5 says "There shall be a Rector of the University who shall be elected by all the matriculated students".

Only after these great honorary offices, from Article 6 onwards, does the Charter go on to list the hired help, starting with the Principal. That is not an accidental running order – for one thing, the Queen by definition does not make mistakes, and for another the order is precisely the same in all the Scottish universities which have Rectors, and is clearly set out as such in successive Universities (Scotland) Acts. But it is an order that this University appears to have mislaid in recent practice. I shall be restoring the influence and the dignity of the position to its rightful place, not for me, but for the reason I am wearing this unembroidered gown – this is based on an undergraduate gown, to indicate that my role is to fight for the interest of the students.

I should be plain that everyone in the University has the welfare of the students at heart – it is simply useful to have someone who has it as their primary concern amid other pressures. One of the problems universitys face is that for funding purposes a prime driver of academic departments is the need to publish a large volume of well reviewed books to produce brownie points. This has led to appalling distortions. You can be a great university academic without ever publishing major research, if you are up with your subject, and communicate knowledge, wisdom and love of the spirit of learning to your students. Cutting edge research provides a key edge to our best teaching, and is a great advantage of many parts of this university. But it is not the sole arbiter of merit, and it is in danger of being so.

My own view – and remember, I have said that a university must be a forum for debate. You don't have to agree with me at all. What you have to do is listen, respect and then engage, from your own perspective and experience.

Nevertheless, my own view is that the University has put too little emphasis on the quality of undergraduate teaching. If you look at The Times' detailed table of university rankings, you will find that our students arrive with a score representing their school qualifications placing us 23rd highest in the UK. We have the 23rd highest qualified people coming in the doors. But our completion rate – those actually achieving their degree – is the 105th best in the country.

You can look up the table yourself. So we have some of the best students arrive, but do poorly on getting them through their degree. Of course, there are statistical anomalies, and the figures vary widely from course to course. But the figures do not lie on overall trend, however you try to spin them, and the truth is that we are not good at value added. Doing better by our undergraduates in this respect will be a major goal of my time as Rector.

Another goal will be to improve the governance of the University. Let me try to illustrate my point visually. These are the minutes of University Court for 91–92. These are the minutes for last academic year. The difference is startling. These are not freak years – you can look at the bound minutes yourselves, and the series gets slimmer and slimmer, with a real step change down around 2001.

That certainly reflects my experience of returning to University Court in 2007 after leaving it in 1984. Minutes are fewer, shorter. The whole Court does not lunch together beforehand now, but rather the Administration cabals with trusties. Decisions are taken outwith Court and without consultation. As Rector, I do not expect to hear of the cutting of a vital student service like the free Ninewells minibus, simply by receiving an email like any member of staff telling me it has already been cut. If the University continue to treat the Rector – and Court – like that, I will continue to embarrass them like this.

The sparsity of the Court minutes is a genuine reflection of the amount of information given to court and the extent Court really takes the decisions. At my first two Court meetings this year I complained that we were being asked to take decisions on cutting academic provision, without having any but the scarcest financial information before us. We were told, for example, that factors in the University being short of money included higher than expected pay awards, an unexpected increase in the cost of energy and increased building costs through a higher cost of steel. I asked for this to be quantified. How much were wage costs estimated, and what was the outturn? How much were energy costs estimated, and what was the outturn? How much had contractors increased the contract by for the higher cost of steel? None of this could be deduced from any of the information given to Court.

Not only did I raise this at two successive Court meetings, without to this day receiving a substantive reply, but the fact that I had asked the question did not appear on either occasion in the minutes. One reason why these volumes are so slim. Dissent is deemed not to happen.

I started some time ago, and I am grateful to you for your patience, by emphasising the need for a University to be a place of free and open debate. Scottish Universities are traditionally democratic self-governing communities, and the election of the Rector is a vital reminder of this. I keep repeating that nobody is obliged to agree with my view, but you should know it. And my view is that the governance of this institution in recent years has been more akin to an old English Polytechnic than a Scottish University.

Let me make plain to you that I believe that under Sir Alan Langlands, this University has blossomed under dynamic and effective leadership which has seen a tremendous expansion, continued cutting edge academic achievement and the introduction of wonderful new facilities, including this one. This has become a truly world-class institution. But I completely reject any notion that the traditional forms of academic community and decision making cannot deliver such results.

Indeed, a wider input can make things better, and too narrow a system of direction can lead to error. I have already mentioned my concern at lack of priority on undergraduate teaching. Another example is this building.

It is a lovely new asset, but it could have been designed twenty years ago. Huge atrium. Central air conditioning. People and Planet conducted a survey of all the UK's universities to rate them for how green they are. We were near the bottom of the list – and you can google that equally true. Look at this building with new eyes. What can you see of the modern innovations in building design which work to offset a building's carbon footprint? What do you think the carbon footprint of this building is? You see what I mean about the need to involve more people. Making this University greener is another of my major aims – because I believe that is in the true interests of the students.

Universities – including this one – have been much afflicted by the cult of right-wing managerialism, exemplified in the view that businessmen are the only people whose expertise is useful and transferable. This goes hand in hand with the obscene view that a business model applies to every form of social interaction and thus social institution. The Scottish Funding Council is packed with businessmen, as is our own University Court. It is worth noting, by the way, that Scottish businessmen are not nowadays renowned for their interest in the cutting edge, as Scottish businesses are in the bottom quartile of OECD tables on percentage of costs spent on research and development.

Now many of those on our Court are excellent people, but they do seem to have a similar perspective on many issues. Wisdom does exist elsewhere in Scotland. In an institution which embraces a great College of Art, it might be good to see a working artist on the Court, more from the professions, journalism, the law, the clergy, the theatre, the arts, the police. A schoolteacher, perhaps. A bit more creative spark. And representatives of all the staff, not only the academics.

Let us reinvigorate the idea of the Scottish democratic community in its universities. We have a great chance now, we a radical government in Edinburgh determined to emphasise all that is best and distinctive in Scottish tradition.

I have a firm proposal to make. I call for the institution of the Scottish tradition of Rectors in all Scottish Universities, not just the ancient ones. I shall be lobbying the Scottish government to take forward this proposal.

Iran Detains British Marines

This incident caused a major outbreak of media jingoism against Iran, which Craig Murray stood against on the grounds of international law. 23 March 2007.

The capture of British Marines by Iran has happened before, then on the Shatt-al-Arab waterway. It will doubtless be used by those seeking to bang the war drum against Iran, though I imagine it will be fairly quickly resolved.

Before people get too carried away, the following is worth bearing in mind. I write as a former Head of the Maritime Section of the Foreign and Commonwealth Office.

The Iranians claimed the British soldiers had strayed into Iranian territorial waters. If they had, then the Iranians had every right to detain them for questioning.

The difficulty is that the maritime delimitation in the North West of the Persian Gulf, between Iraq, Kuwait and Iran, has never been resolved. It is not therefore a question of just checking your GPS to see where you are. This is a perfectly legitimate dispute, in which nobody is particularly at fault. Lateral maritime boundaries from a coastal border point are intensely complicated things, especially where islands and coastal banks become a factor.

Disputes are not unusual. I was personally heavily involved in negotiating British maritime boundaries with Ireland, France and Denmark just ten years ago, and not all our own boundaries are resolved even now. There is nothing outlandish about Iranian claims, and we have no right in law to be boarding Iranian or other shipping in what may well be Iranian waters.

The UN Convention on the Law of The Sea carries a

heavy presumption on the right of commercial vessels to "innocent passage", especially through straits like Hormuz and in both territorial and international waters. You probably won't read this elsewhere in these jingoistic times but, in international law, we are very probably in the wrong. As long as the Iranians neither mistreat our Marines nor wilfully detain them too long, they have the right.

But three days later, he expressed his view that while Iran had the right to arrest the marines, it did not have the right to hold them. His view was for the rule of law, not for either of the parties.

I explained that in international law the Iranian government were not out of order in detaining foreign military personnel in waters to which they have a legitimate claim. For the Royal Navy to be interdicting shipping within the twelve mile limit of territorial seas in a region they know full well is subject to maritime boundary dispute, is unneccessarily provocative. This is especially true as apparently they were not looking for weapons but for smuggled vehicles attempting to evade car duty. What has the evasion of Iranian or Iraqi taxes go to do with the Royal Navy? The ridiculous illogic of the Blair mess gets us further into trouble.

Incidentally, they would under international law have been allowed to enter Iranian territorial waters if in "Hot pursuit" of terrorists, slavers or pirates. But they weren't doing any of those things.

Having said all that, the Iranian authorities, their point made, should now hand the men back immediately. Plainly they were not engaged in piracy or in hostilities against Iran. The Iranians can feel content that they have demonstrated the ability to exercise effective sovereignty over the waters they claim.

Any further detention of the men would now be unlawful and bellicose. One of the great problems facing those of us striving hard to prevent a further disastrous war, this time on Iran, is that the Iranian government is indeed full of theocratic nutters.

His failure to take the "patriotic" side still attracted a great deal of personal criticism, to which he responded by this detailed reiteration of his position on 27 March 2007.

My two earlier posts have caused quite a stir, so here are some further observations.
Sadly, but perhaps predictably, both the British and Iranian governments are now acting like idiots.
Tony Blair has let it be known that he is "utterly confident" that the British personnel were in Iraqi waters. He has of course never been known for his expertise in the Law of the Sea. But let us contrast this political certainty with the actual knowledge of the Royal Navy Commander of the operation on which the captives were taken.
Before the spin doctors could get to him, Commodore Lambert said:
"There is absolutely no doubt in my mind that they were in Iraqi territorial waters. Equally, the Iranians may well claim that they were in their territorial waters. The extent and definition of territorial waters in this part of the world is very complicated".
That is precisely right. The boundary between Iran and Iraq in the northern Persian Gulf has never been fixed. (Within the Shatt-al-Arab itself a line was fixed, but was to be updated every ten years because the waterway shifts, according to the treaty. As it has not been updated in over twenty years, whether it is still valid is a moot point. But it appears this incident occurred well

south of the Shatt anyway.) This is a perfectly legitimate dispute. The existence of this dispute will clearly be indicated on HMS Cornwall's charts, which are in front of Commodore Lambert, but not of Mr Blair.

Until a boundary is agreed, you could only be certain that the personnel were in Iraqi territorial waters if they were within twelve miles of the coast and, at the same time, more than twelve miles from any island, spit, bar or sandbank claimed by Iran (or Kuwait).

That is very hard to judge as the British government refuse to give out the coordinates where the men were captured. If they really are utterly certain, I find that incomprehensible. Everyone knows the Gulf is teeming with British vessels and personnel, so the position of units a few days ago can hardly be valuable intelligence.

Until a boundary is set, it is not easy to posit where it should be. It has to be done by negotiation or arbitration. I have participated in these negotiations, for example on the boundary between the Channel Islands and France.

With a dead straight coastline with no islands, and a dead straight border between two countries hitting the coast at a right angle, you could have a straight maritime border between the two running out from the coast at a right angle. This never happens.

In practice, you agree a series of triangulation points on both coastlines and do a geometric triangulation exercise to find a line running out from the coast. Coasts of course can be very odd shapes. Draw an imaginary coast and border on a bit of paper and try it yourself. You will soon see why the rules permit you to take into account the general trend of the coastline, and even the angle of the land border. Those are not problems of geometry but old fashioned horse trading.

First, of course, both sides will argue about which triangulation points on the coast to accept. You are allowed, for example, to draw a line across a bay entrance and use that as the coast, but there is plenty of room for the other side to argue over where that line is drawn.

That is only the start. For territorial seas (but not the 200 mile exclusive economic zone) uninhabited rocks and sandbanks count. Again huge room for argument here - the ownership of a useless sandbank is not necessarily a settled thing. Sticking your triangulation point on a sandbank twelve miles out can make a huge difference.

Then it really gets complex. What if the sandbank only appears at low tide? What if it is dry all day, but only at certain times of the year? What if it is prone to move about a bit?

You haggle like mad over this. "You can't have that sandbank unless we have this one plus this spit." You also then get into weighting. "That bit of land is only around half the time, so we'll give it one third weighting" - in other words we will allow 33.3% more sea than you would get if it didn't exist and we just used a point on the coast.

Massive volumes have been written on the principles behind these negotiations, but they tend to ignore the fact that ultimately it has to come down to political negotiating skills between a vast range of justifiable possible agreements. That is why we just can't know where the boundary is between Iran and Iraq in this area, which has enough sandbanks to keep me happy thinking about it for centuries. If either side needs a negotiator...

Anyway, the UK was plainly wrong to be ultra provocative in disputed waters. They would be allowed to enter Iranian territorial seas in hot pursuit of terrorists, pirates or slavers, but not to carry out other military operations.

The Iranians had a right to detain the men if they were in seas legitimately claimed as territorial by Iran. Indeed, it is arguable that if a government makes a claim of sovereignty it rather has to enforce it, possession being nine parts of international law. But now the Iranian government is being very foolish, and itself acting illegally, by not releasing the men having made its point.

The story leaked by Russian intelligence claiming knowledge of US plans to attack Iran on 6 April has had great publicity in Iran, if very little here. Personally I doubt it is true. But it seems to me a definite risk that the Iranians will decide to keep the marines against that contingency.

That would be very unfortunate. The Iranian government, by continuing to hold the British personnel, are foolishly providing new impetus to Bush and Blair, whose attempts to bang the war drum against Iran have so far met profound public scepticism. We don't need any more oil wars.

If Blair actually sought the release of our people, rather than anti-Iranian propaganda, he would stop making stupid macho noises and give an assurance that we intend to resolve not only this problem but all disagreements with Iran by peaceful means, and give specific reassurance that no attack is imminent.

But if the Iranian government wait for Blair to behave well, the marines will rot for ever. They should let the men (and woman) go now, with lots of signs of friendship, thus further wrong-footing Bush and Blair.

The British government decided to double down on its claim that the incident had occurred in Iraqi waters, releasing a map which was carried in all broadcast and print media. On 28 March Craig Murray expressed his outrage.

The British Government has published a map showing the coordinates of the incident, well within an Iran/Iraq maritime border. The mainstream media and even the blogosphere has bought this hook, line and sinker.

But there are two colossal problems.

A) The Iran/Iraq maritime boundary shown on the British government map does not exist. It has been drawn up by the British Government. Only Iraq and Iran can agree their bilateral boundary, and they never have done this in the Gulf, only inside the Shatt because there it is the land border too. This published boundary is a fake with no legal force.

B) Accepting the British coordinates for the position of both HMS Cornwall and the incident, both were closer to Iranian land than Iraqi land. Go on, print out the map and measure it. Which underlines the point that the British produced border is not a reliable one.

None of which changes the fact that the Iranians, having made their point, should have handed back the captives immediately. I pray they do so before this thing spirals out of control. But by producing a fake map of the Iran/Iraq boundary, notably unfavourable to Iran, we can only harden the Iranian position.

The next day he responded to concern that the incident could spiral out of control:

There is no agreed maritime boundary between Iraq and Iran in the Persian Gulf. Until the current mad propaganda exercise of the last week, nobody would have found that in the least a controversial statement.

Let me quote, for example, from that well known far left Stars and Stripes magazine, October 24 2006.

"Bumping into the Iranians can't be helped in the northern Persian Gulf, where the lines between Iraqi and Iranian territorial water are blurred", officials said.

"No maritime border has been agreed upon by the two countries," Lockwood said.'

That is Royal Australian Navy Commodore Peter Lockwood. He is the Commander of the Combined Task Force in the Northern Persian Gulf.

I might even know something about it myself, having been Head of the Maritime Section of the Foreign and Commonwealth Office from 1989 to 1992, and having been personally responsible in the Embargo Surveillance Centre for getting individual real time clearance for the Royal Navy to board specific vessels in these waters.

As I feared, Blair adopted the stupid and confrontational approach of publishing maps ignoring the boundary dispute, thus claiming a very blurred situation is crystal clear and the Iranians totally in the wrong. This has in turn notched the Iranians up another twist in their own spiral of intransigence and stupidity.

Both the British and the Iranian governments are milking this for maximum propaganda value and playing to their respective galleries. Neither has any real care at all for either the British captives or the thousands who could die in Iran and Basra if this gets out of hand.

Tony Blair's contempt for Middle Eastern lives has already been adequately demonstrated in Iraq and Lebanon. His lack of genuine concern for British servicemen demonstrated by his steadfast refusal to meet even one parent of a dead British serviceman or woman, killed in the wars he created. He is confronting an Iranian leadership with an equal lust for glory and lack of human concern.

It is essential now for both sides to back down. No solution is possible if either side continues to insist that the other is completely in the wrong and they are completely in the right. And the first step towards finding a peaceful way out, is to acknowledge the self-evident truth that maritime boundaries are disputed and problematic in this area.

Both sides can therefore accept that the other acted in good faith with regard to their view of where the boundary was. They can also accept that boats move about and all the coordinates given by either party were also in good faith. The captives should be immediately released and, to international acclamation, Iran and Iraq, which now are good neighbours, should appoint a joint panel of judges to arbitrate a maritime boundary and settle this boundary dispute.

That is the way out. For the British to insist on their little red border line, or the Iranians on their GPS coordinates, plainly indicates a greater desire to score propaganda points in the run up to a war in which a lot of people will die, than to resolve the dispute and free the captives. The international community needs to put heavy pressure on both Britain and Iran to stop this mad confrontation.

The British people must break out of the jingoism created by their laudable concern for their servicemen and woman, and realise that this is just a small part of the madness of our policy of continual war in the Middle East. That is what we have to stop.

He found himself under attack from a great many directions:

Foreign Policy magazine has a blog which has just published an article calling me a "gadfly" and saying I am "missing the point". The point being a highly contentious statement by former Bahraini government legal adviser Kaiyan Kaikobad that the maritime boundary drawn by the UK MOD has become part of international law by usage.

Actually, I hadn't missed this point at all. Kaikobad's view is quoted in the LA Times, and I spent rather a lot of time explaining to the journalist writing the article what was wrong with his argument. Whether the LA Times carried any of my points I do not know.

The Foreign Policy blog article follows, with the rejoinder I have sent them:

Obviously, the seizure of 15 British marines and sailors and the Iranians' use of them as pawns in a propaganda game is a deadly serious business. Yet there's also plenty of farce amid the danger:

The Iranians also blundered in diplomatic talks by giving the British their own compass reference for the place where they said the 14 men and one woman had been seized. When Britain plotted these on a map and pointed out that the spot was in Iraq's maritime area, the Iranians came up with a new set of coordinates, putting the seizure in their own waters.

Whoops. Turns out, though, that the border issue isn't as black and white as either side claims. King's College of London's Richard Schofield, an expert on the Iran-Iraq border, explained in a telephone interview that although "basically, there is a boundary" nowadays along the Shatt al-Arab, that's not the case further out in the Persian Gulf where the British sailors and marines were taken prisoner. Below is the map presented by the UK Ministry of Defense (MoD):

That's what lends the claims of gadfly Craig Murray, former British ambassador to Uzbekistan, a whiff of plausibility. Murray, who also headed the Maritime Section of the Foreign and Commonwealth Office from 1989 to 1992, writes on his website that "there is no agreed maritime boundary between Iraq and Iran in the Persian Gulf," a milder version of his earlier argument that the boundary used by the MoD "is a fake with no legal force."

Murray is missing the point. True, as Schofield says, "the boundary that [the MoD] showed further south was a little disingenuous, because it doesn't have the same legal force or weighting, by any means, as the Iran-Iraq boundary." Explains Schofield, "It's more just a provisional indication of what Iraq's territorial water claims might be." But what's good for the goose is good for the gander; if there's no clear border, then Iran doesn't have a case, either. And as Kaiyan Kaikobad, an associate professor of international law at Durham University, observes in the LA Times, "If you can show that over a reasonably long period of time, that this was the line that both countries actually agreed on, there's lots of rules in international law that allow that line to become not only a de facto line, but a de jure line." So the MoD could be right after all.

Rather than seizing the opportunity to chalk the whole thing up to a misunderstanding about maritime law, though, the Iranians keep digging themselves into a deeper diplomatic hole, and the British are happy to hand them the shovel. It's clear from the Iranian actions that this isn't really about territorial waters, in any case. After all, the Iranians could have politely notified the British Navy that their boat was in the wrong spot, and the two sides could have worked it out like gentlemen. Instead, we get an absurd hostage situation and a diplomatic crisis. So what's it about? <a href="http://blog.foreignpolicy.com/node/4230">http://blog.foreignpolicy.com/node/4230</a>

I have replied:

I am rather unable to understand why you should be so gratuitously rude about me in your blog, first calling me a "gadfly", then saying that I am "missing the point".

Firstly, I am not missing the point at all - that neither Britain, Iraq nor Iran has a plain case is precisely my point. You give the impression that I support Iranian claims and actions, which I most certainly do not.

Secondly, I am unsure why you should choose to take the view that Kailiyan Kaikobad's view is more valid than the practically identical views of Richard Schofield and I

There are major problems with Kaikobad's view that state practice can result in a de jure as well as a de facto line.

Firstly, there are no judgments that enshrine that view in the area of maritime boundaries since the UN Convention on the Law of the Sea entered into force.

Secondly UNCLOS provides that, in the absence of an agreed boundary, neither side should attempt to enforce territorial water claims beyond a median line. It is very plain that this is for the purpose of conflict avoidance, and does not prejudice either state's rights in the eventual resolution of the boundary dispute.

So Kaikobad's view that working accommodation does bring de jure permanent solution is incompatible with UNCLOS, which is becoming generally accepted as enshrining customary international law in this area.

Thirdly, the wisdom of UNCLOS in this regard is demonstrated if you consider the ramifications of Kaikobad's view. If going along with a working arrangement would lead to its acceptance as de jure, then the only way a state could maintain a quite legitimate claim would be by the exercise of force to show it did not go along. Kaikobad's view is a recipe for conflict. If you think about it logically, if Kaikobad's view were true, then the Iranians would have to initiate some sort of military action or lose their claim. Is that desirable?

Kaikobad is an interesting man of strong views, but not an entirely definitive authority.

Look, it is a free country and you are perfectly entitled to publish about me what you like. But to disagree with a point is not to miss it, and I hope this convinces you that was an unfair characterisation.

By 1 April, with the marines still held captive and the original fervour dying down, he was able to get more of a hearing.

Firstly, many thanks to the Mail on Sunday for being the first bit of the mainstream media ready to give a fair hearing to what I have been saying, and to try and understand the situation rather than just belt out propaganda.
At a working level, Whitehall is trying to get reality back into the British position, though this may get stomped on again by the spin doctors. One of my many friends within the FCO has seen minutes between officials discussing "Craig Murray's points" on the border question and whether admitting the border is unclear could be a path to getting our people back (Freedom of Information request for that minuting, anyone?).
The Observer today gives the first hint that the MOD may be looking to backtrack on its unsustainable border claims:
"But the Ministry of Defence hinted for the first time it may have made mistakes surrounding the incident. An inquiry has been commissioned to explore 'navigational' issues around the kidnapping and aspects of maritime law."

The plain truth of his argument as a matter of fact was starting to be realised:

In today's printed version of the Sueddeutsche Zeitung, Prof Khan of the University for the Federal Armed Forces in Munich confirms Craig Murray's statement:
"In their presentation, the British have effectively drawn a fictitious line in their attempt to prove where exactly the soldiers were when taken captive instead of showing

a clear border. They couldn't have done the latter in any case as the border between Iran and Iraq around Shatt el-Arab is not clearly identifiable."

The more he dug, the more problems he found:

Let me start by saying that I am not querying the coordinates (29 degrees 50.36 minutes North 048 degrees 43.08 minutes East) for the Indian merchant vessel given by the UK MOD. In the British version the incident took place at that vessel. They said that the Indian vessel was anchored at these coordinates for two days.

By contrast the Iranian government has given four different coordinates, allegedly referring not to a single incident but to the course of the Royal Naval vessels.

My point has been all along that the precise coordinates are a red herring, because the maritime boundary has never been agreed. There is therefore no clear "line" you can be one side or the other of.

But I have been contacted now by three independent people - two claiming experience as mariners - to make the following point. To the best of my ability I have checked it out, but I am not a qualified navigator. I am not claiming that the following is correct - it is put forward as a problem, not a solution. I am appealing for assistance from those technically equipped to throw any light on this problem.

The MOD claimed that the Indian merchant vessel was anchored "in the channel". But these coordinates are over a nautical mile further West (ie towards Iraq) than the channel. That bit I am quite certain of.

The mystery is this. On British nautical maps, 29 degrees 50.36 minutes North 048 degrees 43.08 minutes East is 100 yards above the low water line. That is to say it dries out at low tide. The vessel pictured by the MOD is a substantial merchant vessel. No captain of such a vessel would knowingly take his vessel to such a position, let alone anchor it there for two days.

In fact legally speaking, those coordinates are on land.

As always, it is a bit more complex than that. British charts use the Lowest Astronomical Tide - that is the furthest the tide normally goes out in a year. So on British charts the vessel is 100 yards above the low water mark when the tide is at its lowest. US charts, which show a more normal low tide, show it as being just below the low water line. But that still puts it in very shallow water indeed.

Consider this. There is very little tide in the Gulf. The highest tidal range there is a vertical fall of only nine feet, and that is closer to the Arabian sea. Perhaps someone can find the draught of the Indian vessel when it left port (Lloyds List should have this). But it was laden with cars. I cannot conceive of it having a draught of less than twelve feet, possibly a good lot more.

In short, unless I am missing something very important, it looks like it would be very hard to get that Indian vessel to those coordinates at high tide, and it would certainly ground at low tide, pretty well at any time of year.

Before we leap to any conclusions, I can see at least three other possible explanations:

The mud and sands have shifted substantially since the charts were made, or it has been radically dredged

Sea levels in the Gulf at the time in question were, for some reason, unusually high; perhaps with some very local effect from very high outflow from the rivers

Neither the people who contacted me nor I can read a chart properly

What I am looking for are technical contributions to explain the alleged problem. Until we have clarified that, I would be grateful if the political pundits could hold fire. I am not saying that the coordinates were wrong, or that the ship could not be in that position.

Almost single-handedly, he had turned the tide of media opinion on the incident, but there were scars:

It has been a very hectic few days, but they have been productive. I seem to have helped convince the mainstream media of the obvious truth that the maritime boundaries in this part of the Gulf are disputed and fuzzy, and that the real situation is much less clear than the British map. The BBC has at last started routinely to refer to the boundary as disputed and unclear. The support from the Mail on Sunday and Daily Mail helped enormously to turn the tide, as did the serious piece in the New York Times.

Last night I did Newsnight, BBC News 24 and a pre-record for this morning's Breakfast TV. In all cases the BBC introduction stated that the border was disputed and complex as reported fact before I started, which made it much easier.

This morning Richard Dalton, former British Ambassador to Iran, said clearly on BBC Breakfast TV that nobody could be certain whose waters they were in, that the boundary is not agreed and negotiating such boundaries is very complex. That is the first open confirmation of this from an "Establishment" figure since the Blair spin about being "utterly certain" we were in Iraqi waters.

Furthermore, both the FCO and MOD appear to have cottoned on that accepting this as all a muddle is the wiggle room for diplomacy to get us out of this dispute with neither side losing too much face, and the way to get our people back quickly.

There is always something of a price to pay for standing up to the government. I am Rector of the University of Dundee. The local newspaper, the Courier and

Advertiser, yesterday published an article giving a highly tendentious account of my views, making me out to support the Iranian detention of the sailors. I wrote a letter to the Editor for publication to correct this, in mild terms, and telephoned yesterday afternoon to check they had received it. They did not publish my letter, but today published an article saying that students were calling for my resignation over my views on Iran. They still have made no effort to talk to me or get my view.

This is the letter I sent to the Courier.

> Sir,
>
> I feel your report today (2 April) was remiss in not noting that I am calling for Iran to hand the captives back immediately, and have made that call consistently since the incident started. You seem to wish to portray me as supporting Iran in this affair, which is completely unfair. I want both sides to see sense and solve this peacefully and very quickly.
>
> There is no agreed Iran/Iraq boundary in the Gulf south of the Shatt al Arab river. That is not a "claim" by me, it is an undeniable fact. Maritime boundaries are established by treaty, and there has never been one. Doubtless the Law department of the University, which had always been very good on international maritime law, can confirm that for you.
>
> The incident took place in disputed waters. That is all we can say. It is also all we were saying. Commodore Tim Lambert on HMS Cornwall stated just after the incident: "There is absolutely no doubt in my mind that we were in Iraqi territorial waters. Equally the Iranians may well claim that they were in their territorial waters. The extent and definition of territorial waters in this part of the world is very complicated."
>
> Commodore Lambert summed the real situation up perfectly. But then the Number 10 spin doctors got to

work and Tony Blair made the fatuous claim that he was "Utterly certain" that the incident was in Iraqi territorial waters. The MOD backed this up by producing a map showing a boundary in bright red lines. That boundary does not exist - it was drawn up by the MOD.

By publishing a map purporting to set the boundary in the Gulf, we closed the door on the obvious way to resolve this dispute and turned an incident into a crisis. The government's desire to make hay out of jingoistic propaganda exceeded its desire to find a solution which would see our personnel returned.

The Iranians have legitimate claims in these seas - as do the Iraqis. it is not for us to decide the boundary between them. For the Iranians to make a practical demonstration of their claim against a foreign power boarding vessels in what they claim as "their" waters is arguably justifiable. But given the waters are disputed, they should behave with much greater circumspection, and to hold captives is bellicose and unjustified.

Both governments have painted themselves into corners. Both have to back down. The way to do that is to admit what everybody knew until they forgot it last week, that these waters are disputed and nobody knows for sure where the boundary is. We make plain that we had no intention of straying into Iranian territorial waters. The Iranians let our people go.

This should not be difficult to solve if the governments involved act reasonably. Both countries have leaderships which are deeply unpopular at home. The danger in those circumstances is that politicians welcome a chance to bang the drum of jingoism to win votes at home, and are disinclined to compromise. I see elements of that here, and fear for our captives.

One element of this political trick is to pretend there are only two positions, and that anyone who queries is a "traitor" and on the side of the "enemy". I am on the side of humanity.

Craig Murray

On the brighter side, I always find Jeremy Paxman instinctively likable when I meet him. I realise that is not a universal view. Just before we went on air, he said that since I last met him he had read, and greatly enjoyed, Murder in Samarkand. I always feel a real thrill when anyone says they read it. I can't quite explain why - it feels like they must really know me, so we have got through at least one side of several year's worth of making friends before we start.

I confess to being a bit disappointed by sales of the book. It has sold some 8,000 in hardback, while the paperback has only been out for six weeks so it is a bit early to tell. I had unrealistic dreams of selling huge quantities - everyone tells me that 8,000 hardbacks for non-fiction is really good. But it certainly isn't enough to live on - I get around 8% of the cover price, minus the costs of the map, index, some legal costs etc. Work it out.

What I find hard to reconcile is the astonishingly positive reaction from those who have read it, with the fairly low sales. I say astonishingly positive because so far 317 complete strangers (yes, I know, I am very nerdish to keep count) who have read Murder in Samarkand have emailed me to say what a huge impact it had on them. There seem two main themes - people did not realise how dark and despicable the heart of our government really is, and people relate to the open account of my own faults and eventual disintegration. Especially the letters indicate anyone who has ever suffered injustice from government or an unfair employer, seems to find those emotional wounds reopened.

But the book does not tell you how to contact me. I don't think it would ever occur to me to contact the author of a book I had read. Yet 317 people who, with a very few exceptions, appear perfectly sane, have read Murder in Samarkand and then gone to the length of looking up my website, finding my contact details, and then writing to give me their reactions to my book.

The other thing that seems very positive is the number of very famous people who have now read it. I can only name those I happen to know have done so - until last night, for example, I had no idea Jeremy Paxman had. This is a bit of unashamed name-dropping, but among those I know have read Murder in Samarkand are: Noam Chomsky, Harold Pinter, David Owen, Brad Pitt, Tony Benn, David Frost, Jeremy Paxman, Bianca Jagger, David Hare and Steve Coogan.

So I am left wondering why it is not selling better. I think that part of the problem is marketing. If you go into Waterstones or Borders, you will probably find a copy, but you will have to go up or down to the politics department and poke around the bottom shelves until you find a single copy, spine-on. To sell well nowadays, a book has to be on tables in a "3 for 2" promotion or similar. For that your publisher has to do a deal with the bookstore - one of the disastrous results of independent booksellers being replaced by big chains. My publisher, Mainstream, uses Random House for its distribution and marketing. When asked why they didn't make more effort to promote the book, Random House replied (I paraphrase, but not much) "Because nobody's ever heard of Craig Murray".

All of which is very frustrating. But the book is out there, and spreading solely by word of mouth. The emails keep coming in, and keep my spirits up hugely.

Finally on 5 April the marines were released by the Iranians

Any life saved is a victory, and I am delighted that the maritime incident has been resolved with nobody being killed or even injured. That is the right perspective on this.

Today four more unfortunate British serviceman died in Southern Iraq as a result of Blair's crass Middle Eastern policy. Think of them and their families, and the seventy Iraqi civilians who on average will be killed today. Yes, rejoice at the fifteen who came home safely today, but remember those who did not, and their families.

Less than a week before this fifteen were captured, the media received the confirmation that British government scientists believed that 655,000 dead in Iraq a year ago was a good estimate. That received almost no press coverage. The detention of fifteen Britons for ten days is more important than the agonising deaths of hundreds of thousands of Iraqis.

There was a revelatory moment on BBC Breakfast TV this morning when Admiral Sir Alan West said he was sure we had been in "our" waters. He corrected himself afterwards to "Iraqi waters" but the slip reveals the mindset of the occupying forces.

It is an extraordinarily wide interpretation of the UN occupation mandate to use it to interdict neutral merchant shipping in the Gulf. For me one of the most amazing things about this sorry dispute is that HMS Cornwall was, by the MOD's own account and according to the embedded journalists on board, attempting to prevent the smuggling of cars. Am I really paying my taxes for incredibly sophisticated warships to be involved in the collection of Iraqi vehicle excise duty?

The Iranian release caught the UK on the hop and was a political coup, but followed British diplomacy offering technical talks on the disputed boundary area and the conduct of future operations. I hope that in the not too distant future Iran and Iraq will negotiate their maritime border; but thanks to us Iraq has a government that controls a tiny proportion of its land, let alone its seas.

Let us hope that the safe return of the fifteen shall be followed swiftly by the safe return of all our forces. They should never have been there in the first place.

He added a coda the same day:

I just heard the Iraqi Foreign Minister on BBC Radio "The World at One".

He said "That border is disputed. It has been for many years. It has moved. That is why we had this war of maps...We have agreed with Iran that our technical levels will fix this border including in the Shatt-al-Arab."'

Interestingly he said that the Iraqi government had asked the US government, several weeks ago, to release the five Iranians captured by US troops. The US is "reviewing the request".

There could be no clearer illustration that the idea that Iraq has a sovereign government is a sham. That the Iraqi government is not able to stop the US, against its will, capturing and imprisoning foreigners on the territory of Iraq, is sufficient proof that Iraq remains a state under hostile occupation.

How do those who claim that we are in Iraq under a UN mandate to assist the Iraqi government, square this with the exercise of physical force and deprival of liberty by US forces against the express will of the so-called government of the country?

All this resulted in some interesting broadcast media exposure.

I had the interesting experience of sitting on set at BBC News 24 for over an hour today, intermittently talking and intermittently on camera. I had come in to discuss both the maritime boundaries issue and the question of the behind the scenes diplomatic negotiations. As Oliver Miles said today, there were at least ten bilateral discussions between Iran and British ambassadors, ministers and No 10 officials. Tony Blair might claim there were no negotiations, but they weren't discussing the weather.

Anyway, I was on air when the hostages arrived by helicopter and were reunited with their families. Thus I found myself being asked for an hour questions such as "How do you think the families are feeling?"

I should say that the presenters were really nice, and the hectic atmosphere of a newsroom on a big live breaking story is great fun. I found myself involved in an interesting game of offering deadpan expert analysis, but interspersing it with subversive comment. I didn't want to push that too hard or I was pretty plain I would have got yanked off. So over the course of an hour I first slipped in the observation that, as a taxpayer, I was not too keen on financing very expensive warships steaming around the Gulf allegedly to collect vehicle excise duty. Later I was able to say that, while I shared the unalloyed delight at the return of the 15, I was thinking rather more about the families of the four British servicemen who had been killed in Iraq today, and their civilian interpreter. Before they could recover from the shock of that burst through the reverential coverage, I added the 70 Iraqi civilians who on average die every day.

You should understand that over the long broadcast I mostly talked about the return of the captives and had no difficulty in being genuinely upbeat and happy about that. But the reunion of captives and families probably had the largest live news audience for many months; it did not escape the No 10 spin doctors' attention that their "Triumph for Tony" moment was being jeopardised by a dissident having been allowed on the BBC.

Ask yourself - when is the last time you saw an anti-war voice, as opposed to a pro-war "military" or "security" expert, asked by the BBC to comment on a Middle East development? Yet the majority of people in this country are against the war. If they want an ex-diplomat, they go for pro war cheerleaders Pauline Neville Jones or Christopher Meyer, even though eight out of ten ex British Ambassadors are against the war.

Anyway the outraged phone calls from the government to the BBC started coming in. As a result, having been introduced as "Former Head of the Foreign Office Maritime Section and Former British Ambassador..." the first time, I was reintroduced as "Craig Murray, who was sacked as British Ambassador to Uzbekistan for opposing British government policy". The poor presenters, with whom I had been getting on well for an hour, seemed embarrassed

I therefore decided the gloves were off, and introduced "the elephant in the room - that the large majority of the British people don't believe that our servicemen should be in Iraq and in harm's way in the first place."

There is no doubt at all that when you make anti-war or anti-government points on the BBC the whole body language and line of questioning indicates that you are some sort of isolated extremist. Of course, our so called opposition parties fail to make any such points, and the BBC's normal pool of experts are hand picked to be reliably right wing on these issues. The absolutely astonishing thing is that I then whizzed off to Sky News (Fox affiliate) and there, in the heart of the Murdoch

Empire, the atmosphere is totally different.

I was asked open questions if anything leading me on to be overtly critical of the war, Tony Blair and John Bolton. This is not unusual. Tony Benn, George Galloway and I all get far easier access to Sky than the BBC. Sky does seem to maintain a modicum of journalistic integrity. The BBC has totally lost it since Gilligan, Dyke and Hussey were sacked for telling the truth about Iraqi WMD, and David Kelly was murdered.

Anyway, after Sky I went to buy a birthday present for Nadira. A lady outside the shop told me that she had just seen me on the TV. "I used to listen to you on Radio 4" she said, "You looked a lot better on the radio."

My Week

An edited version of this column was published as the regular "my week" column in the Observer magazine.

It is interesting to compare what they published with what I submitted. Shortened for length, obviously, but the editing makes it look like my comments on alcohol were a jibe at Muslims, when in fact they were a jibe at Nick Cohen. It is perhaps understandable that the Observer have taken out criticism of their long-standing columnist and new neo-con pin-up. Slightly more worrying that they didn't think my attack on the appointment of an appalling New Labour hack as chairman of the BBC was worth printing:

Nadira is studying a postgraduate acting course at Drama Studio London, an acting school of very high reputation. They have just broken up for Easter, and I go along to their end of term karaoke party. I feel inspirited by these young people. I would like to sing but Nadira only took me along after I promised I wouldn't. Interestingly they all choose songs from my generation, not theirs. I learn that a song I have heard on a hundred radios, but didn't know the title, is called 'La Isla Bonita' or sometimes, on this karaoke machine, 'La Isla Bonita'. Does the Guardian do karaoke machines? Anyway one line in this song had always startled me. 'I fell in love with some dago' had always seemed a strange thing to sing, even in less politically correct times. I now see on the machine it was San Pedro she fell in love with: presumably a place not a holy old fisherman.
I also discovered that the Abba line from Super Trouper is not the improbable 'Since I called you last night from Tesco' but rather 'Glasgow'.

Which is, of course, even less romantic.

I have spent a great deal of the week dashing between television and radio studios to give interviews about the Iran captives. I used to be head of the Maritime Section of the Foreign Office. In the first Gulf War I lived, quite literally, in an underground bunker working in the Embargo Surveillance Centre. I worked with Naval staff and was very heavily involved in the real time direction of Gulf interdiction operations. So I really know about this stuff.

There were farcical elements to the whole incident. Neither the British, Iraqis nor Iranians could say whose waters they were in, as the boundaries have never been agreed outside the Shatt-al-Arab. The military failure was due to the fact we have nothing in the area between a warship and a rubber dinghy; it reminded me of the Cod War with Iceland all over again (we lost that one too). Still less can I understand why we have warships attempting to collect Iraqi vehicle excise duty. These patrols, maintained at enormous expense to the British taxpayer, have made precisely zero seizures of significant quantities of explosives or guns. Up the Gulf by ship is not how the insurgents are supplied. The looting of thousands of tonnes of munitions from the disbanded Iraqi army was enough to keep them going for many years.

An extraordinary thing is the disconnect between the BBC presentation and what ordinary people can see. I think I can honestly claim that, unless you happened to catch me being interviewed, nothing else in hundreds of hours of BBC TV coverage would give a stranger the slightest clue that the majority of British people do not think our troops and Navy should be there in the first place. I am genuinely sorry for the ideal of these young people, but nobody can pretend it was a patch on extraordinary rendition to an Uzbek dungeon, on

Guantanamo Bay, Abu Ghraib or the regular beating of Iraqi prisoners by British troops, of which the hideous murder of Baha Musa is just one very bad example. There was infinitely more focus on the rejoicing families of our returned captives than there was thought for the grieving families of the four men and women just killed. Having sent those young people to their useless deaths, Blair's only thought was to use them to bang the drum further for war against Iran,

Ask yourself - when is the last time you saw an anti-war voice, as opposed to a pro-war "military" or "security" expert, asked by the BBC to comment on a Middle East development? Yet the majority of people in this country are against the war. If they want an ex-diplomat, they go for pro war cheerleaders Pauline Neville Jones or Christopher Meyer, even though eight out of ten ex British Ambassadors are against the war.

Amazingly, Sky News is much more open to dissent, and gives much fairer representation to anti-war voices, than the BBC. I see that a New Labour apparatchik and mate of Gordon Brown has just been appointed to chair that august body. There would be no danger now of any unfortunate outbreak of the truth on the BBC, as when Andrew Gilligan told the nation there were no Iraqi WMD.

Lunch with Michael Winterbottom and Andrew Eaton to discuss the latest developments in producing the film of Murder in Samarkand, the book of my time in Uzbekistan. Paramount are funding the project and it is good to discuss filming locations and casting with a pretty open budget. There has been a change of writer since we last met, and Michael himself has drawn up the 'treatment.' We agree that the drama has to be griping, the sex erotic and the humour hilarious. Michael has a passion for authenticity which could cause problems. He is very insistent, for example, that Uzbeks should play

Uzbeks and Russians play Russians. I point out that this is no problem provided we can find actors with no objection to be executed or murdered by their governments once the film is shown.

Steve Coogan is to play me. He is, of course, not nearly good looking enough. But then, who is?

This week I read 'An Honorable Deception' by Clare Short, and 'What's Left' by Nick Cohen. I confess to being a fan of Clare Short. Unfortunately her on/off resignation did huge damage to her standing, and probably to the sales of this book. That is a great pity because what it has to say about the sickness at the heart of New Labour is quite devastating.

Let me summarise Nick Cohen's book for you. 'If you are against eating Muslim babies, you are a supporter of Islamofascism. If you are perturbed by Guantanamo Bay, you would not have fought in the Spanish Civil War, are probably a fan of Hitler and have no right to call yourself a Liberal. Neo-Conservatism is the New Left.'

There, now you don't have to read it. Believe me, I have done you a favour.

I have never been much attracted to Islam myself as my hobbies are drinking whisky and chasing women. Contrary to Cohen's argument, the very many British Muslims I know, some of them very radical, have no problems with my lifestyle or any intention of imposing their religion on the rest of the UK.

I think the fight against neo-puritanism is very important. The mineral water at lunch crew are a fundamental threat to civilisation. I have always maintained stoutly that it is possible to drink a great deal without any impairment of the mental faculties. I fear Cohen's book may be disproving that.

I am making arrangements to get to Ghana for the funeral of my friend, Hawa Yakubu. Hawa was a woman of quite extraordinary influence across West Africa. She was on the closest terms with almost every major African Head of State over thirty years. I recall late one night we were struggling with ideas in the negotiations for the Sierra Leone peace treaty, and she simply phoned President Obasanjo of Nigeria at 2am to ask him to put pressure on Charles Taylor. It says volumes about Hawa that he was delighted to be awoken by his old friend.

Hawa did huge amounts for women's development, for African integration, for conservation, and for the poverty-stricken West African Savannah Belt. She was completely non-corrupt and leaves no personal fortune. Her influence was absolutely vital in helping Ghana become a democracy after Rawlings. She never held more than junior ministerial office because she found it too limiting. One of the most positive influences bringing hope to modern Africa, she is mourned by an extraordinary number of powerful people on several continents. It says much of our modern remoteness from African affairs that no British media have noted her passing.

Good Friday is Nadira's birthday. Foxy, our cat, gave birth to four kittens. Last year on Nadira's birthday Foxy gave birth to one, Chocolate, who we still have. Nadira goes all gooey-eyed on me and insists we must keep the kittens. I point out that our long-suffering landlord, Mr Dash, has already put up with two cats when our lease clearly states that we are allowed no pets.

'But you don't have any money to pay the rent anyway, so why would he worry about a few kittens?' Nadira asks. I don't see how to argue with that.

Yeltsin's Funeral

With his unrivalled capacity for being in the right place at the right time quite by accident, Craig Murray found himself mingling with the crowds at Yeltsin's funeral on 25 April 2007.

I have been busy with anti-war meetings in Edinburgh and Glasgow at the weekend, and then to Dundee for a University Court meeting on Monday, with lots of pre- and post-consultations. Got back home at 1.30am Tuesday (because the University values its Rector so highly it insists he travels Easyjet). Then quite literally up all night dealing with correspondence, and an 08.55 flight from Heathrow. Now blogging from Moscow. Couldn't resist the chance to mingle with the crowds at Yeltsin's funeral. Astonished by how pinched and old Clinton looks - George Bush senior appears hale. The UK sends the Z team - Prince Andrew and John Major. Not so much damning with faint praise, as faint greys.

I am impressed by the many thousands of Muscovites, filing past the coffin all night and lining the short funeral route. I vox pop the funeral crowds, who are of course a self-selecting biased sample, but the Western media seems rather too glibly to accept the line from the state controlled Russian media that Yeltsin's mistakes are remembered more than his achievements. At night I wander down to the White House and look at the cars whizzing past, over the spot where he climbed on the armoured vehicle (not actually a tank) to save Russian democracy and prevent the restoration of Soviet dictatorship. John Major is not really inappropriate as a mourner, because he had been speaking to Yeltsin from London moments before he did that. It is worth remembering that the troops had opened fire. Major says Yeltsin genuinely thought he would die then.

The media talk of Yeltsin as Russia's first democratic President. I fear "only" might be a better word than first. Certainly mistakes were made in the uncontrolled rush to capitalism, as Abramovich and his like looted the country. It was done much better in Central Europe, with voucher schemes and other ways to get some immediate benefit to ordinary people. But hindsight is a wonderful thing, and it must not be forgotten how fragile the new Russian revolution was, and how real at first was the fear of Soviet resurgence. There was reason to hurry.

That does not excuse the ensuing creation of robber barons or Yeltsin's decline into a drunken, jovial tool of corruption. But he had many decent human qualities, one of which was a lack of arrogance. Nobody noticed his resignation as President because it was the Millennium and we were all getting pissed. But he apologised to the Russian people for his mistakes, and especially the Chechen war. Do not expect Blair to follow.

Outside the White House is a girl with short blonde hair carrying two red roses. She too is looking at the road and thinking of Yeltsin. I point out that with today's traffic, the army would never have got there. She has tears in her eyes - "He gave us our freedom". She is bitterly amused that the only other person who thought to go to the White House on this evening is a passing Scot. I tell her she looks too young to remember all this. She says she was in her first year at University when he resigned. But she remembers the White House, as a child. "He used to be handsome".

We go for a pizza - thus adding a new tactic to my range of pick-up techniques. In the "Golden Drum" pub, the consensus is that at least Yeltsin ended Gorbachev's anti-alcohol drive. His memory fades in a night of beer and vodka. Perhaps he wouldn't mind that.

Zionism is Bullshit

Printed in Great Britain
by Amazon